TRIKALYAM | PREM NATH | GOLDEN PALMS | CITIMALL | RAJINDER KUMAR | INDIA EXPO MART LTD | ITC GREEN CENTRE | REZA KABUL | RAGHULEELA MALL | SHIRAZI MOSQUE | SP PATKI | THE OBEROI AMARVILAS | OSHO COMMUNE | SANJAY PURI | AMBY VALLEY LEISURE CENTRE | KALPATARU HORIZON | SHASHI PRABHU | SHIVAJI CHATRAPATI SPORTS CITY | LILAVATI HOSPITAL | YATIN PATEL | I-FLEX | LOGICA CMG | CN RAGHAVENDRAN | COGNIZANT | EBENE CYBER TOWERS | HAFEEZ CONTRACTOR | INFOSYS | ADITYA BIRLA HQ | JP AGARWAL | TECHNOPOLIS | INFINITY | KAMAL MALIK | LUPIN RESEARCH CENTRE | INSTITUTE OF ONCOLOGICAL SCIENCES | KARAN GROVER | CII SHORABJI GBC | CII ABB INSTITUTE | NIMISH CHOKSI | BABULAL SANGHVI RESIDENCE | TIMBER VALLEY | NITEEN PARULEKAR | EON | SYNTEL | NITIN KILLAWALA | NICHOLAS PIRAMAL RESEARCH CENTRE

VERSATILE INDIAN
ARCHITECTS

COVER: The Oberoi Amarvilas by S P Patki (Courtesy Oberoi Hotels & Resorts)
TITLE & CONTENT PAGE: Lupin Research Centre by Kamal S Malik (Courtesy Bharath Ramamrutham)

COMPILED BY
White Flag Media & Communications Ltd

ART DIRECTION & DESIGN
Kena Design, Bengaluru
www.kenadesign.com

IMAGE & TEXT EDITING
Kena Design, Bengaluru
www.kenadesign.com

PRINTED BY
JAK Printers, Mumbai

PUBLISHED BY
© White Flag Media & Communications Ltd
173 / 174, Sezal Encasa, S V Road, Kandivali (W)
Mumbai 400067, India
Tel: +91 22 28665100, Fax: +91 22 28665102
Email: info@whiteflag.co.in
www.whiteflag.co.in

FIRST PUBLISHED IN 2011

ISBN
978-81-908789-0-6

VERSATILE INDIAN
ARCHITECTS

Rising with ideas

Published by White Flag

contents

FIRM NAME
C R Narayana Rao & Associates

ADDRESS
10, Karpagambal Nagar
Mylapore
Chennai 600014
Tamil Nadu

CONTACT
Tel: +91 44 24991676
www.crn.co.in

Today's children don't have the privilege to be just children. Space constraints and other pressures force them to become adults very soon]

01 C N RAGHAVENDRAN

Born in 1944 to Civil Engineer C R Narayana Rao, C N Raghavendran completed his primary and secondary education in Chennai. Apart from studies, Raghavendran's childhood was spent playing hockey, football and cricket with his friends and family. After successfully completing his pre-university course from Vivekananda College, Chennai, Raghavendran went to study Architecture at Indian Institute of Technology, Kharagpur. Following his graduation, he worked with his father for almost a year, before attending University of California, Berkeley, for postgraduate studies in Architecture. He joined his father's firm C R Narayana Rao & Associates upon returning to India with M. Arch. from Berkeley, USA. Over the last 6 decades, their firm has gained immense recognition and expanded their business to cover all the 4 states in Southern India. As early as 1960s, the firm gained recognition for their innovative architecture for the prestigious Dunlop and Ashok Leyland factories. Besides industrial projects, the firm has also designed many educational institutions, textile mills and sports stadiums. Their loyal clients include some of India's large scale global companies like Infosys, TCS, Wipro, Satyam, HCL, Oracle and Computer Associates among others. A landmark achievement for this firm has been the construction of Tidel Park, a 1.5 million sft building equipped with energy saving measures. A one-of-its-kind energy efficient building, it was inaugurated and praised by the then Prime Minister of India. With a 250-strong team of dedicated employees, the two brothers, C N Raghavendran and Dr C N Srinivasan are giving face to many dreams.

CLIENT
Cognizant Technology Solutions India Pvt Ltd

CATEGORY
Single Occupancy Information Technology Park

LOCATION
Chennai, Tamil Nadu

PRINCIPAL ARCHITECT
C N Raghavendran

DESIGN TEAM
L Venkatesh
N K Manee
N Seshadri
C Sambabu Manohar

CONTRACTORS
Larsen & Toubro (ECC)

STRUCTURAL, MECHANICAL & ELECTRICAL
C R Narayana Rao Architects & Engineers

LANDSCAPE ARCHITECTS
Master Plan

PROJECT DATE
2002 – 2003

1.01 COGNIZANT

A multinational IT company with development centres in Chennai, Pune, Kolkata, Hyderabad and Bengaluru, Cognizant's Chennai office has been designed to give its employees a healthy working space and provide a smart face to its potential clients. This Chennai centre is also aimed to be a business house, which communicates trust, capability and clarity in its vision to all its users and visitors. It is a state-of-the-art building designed to meet the most demanding 24/7/365 needs of a global ICT operator. C N Raghavendran is the principal architect of this project who designed this centre along with his team to align with Cognizant's corporate image. The architecture supports the demands of a rapidly changing digital global economy while integrating an ambience to inspire zest and energy. The plan has been formulated to house two development centres, Software Development Blocks (SDB) I and II. This forms the core working area of the company. The other two buildings house the canteen and an academy for training and e-learning centres.

1.01 COGNIZANT

The design enables all the buildings a north-south exposure to limit the effect of the solar heat gains. To further integrate the buildings visually and provide a relief from the large volumes, the ground level is extensively landscaped. The landscaped area provides a very striking geometry which is visible from within the buildings, the green spaces rise as floating gardens at the ground level and provides a visual continuity as one moves through the campus. The contrasting colours of the shrubs, trees and flower beds provide an unforgettable visual medley. The reception area is an explosive burst of vast three-dimensional space defined by the solid mass of the blue clad walls, which reflect below on the polish of the Italian marble floors creating an ambience, which is powerful but not dominating. The entrance wall with its state-of-the-art stainless steel forged glass brackets (called 'Spider Glazing') is the skin, which allows the buildings to breathe by seamlessly integrating the interior spaces with the external dimensions. One important and striking aspect of this project is the IBMS system. This nerve centre is located in SDB-II and from here, every building utility is controlled over the Cognizant network. No aspect of the building escapes attention of this advanced monitoring system. The plan also includes facilities for the disabled, which showcases the company's employee-friendly policies and the architect's thoughtful solutions. This centre has gained instant recognition as one of the most employee-friendly, functional, sleek and state-of-the-art facility.

SITE PLAN

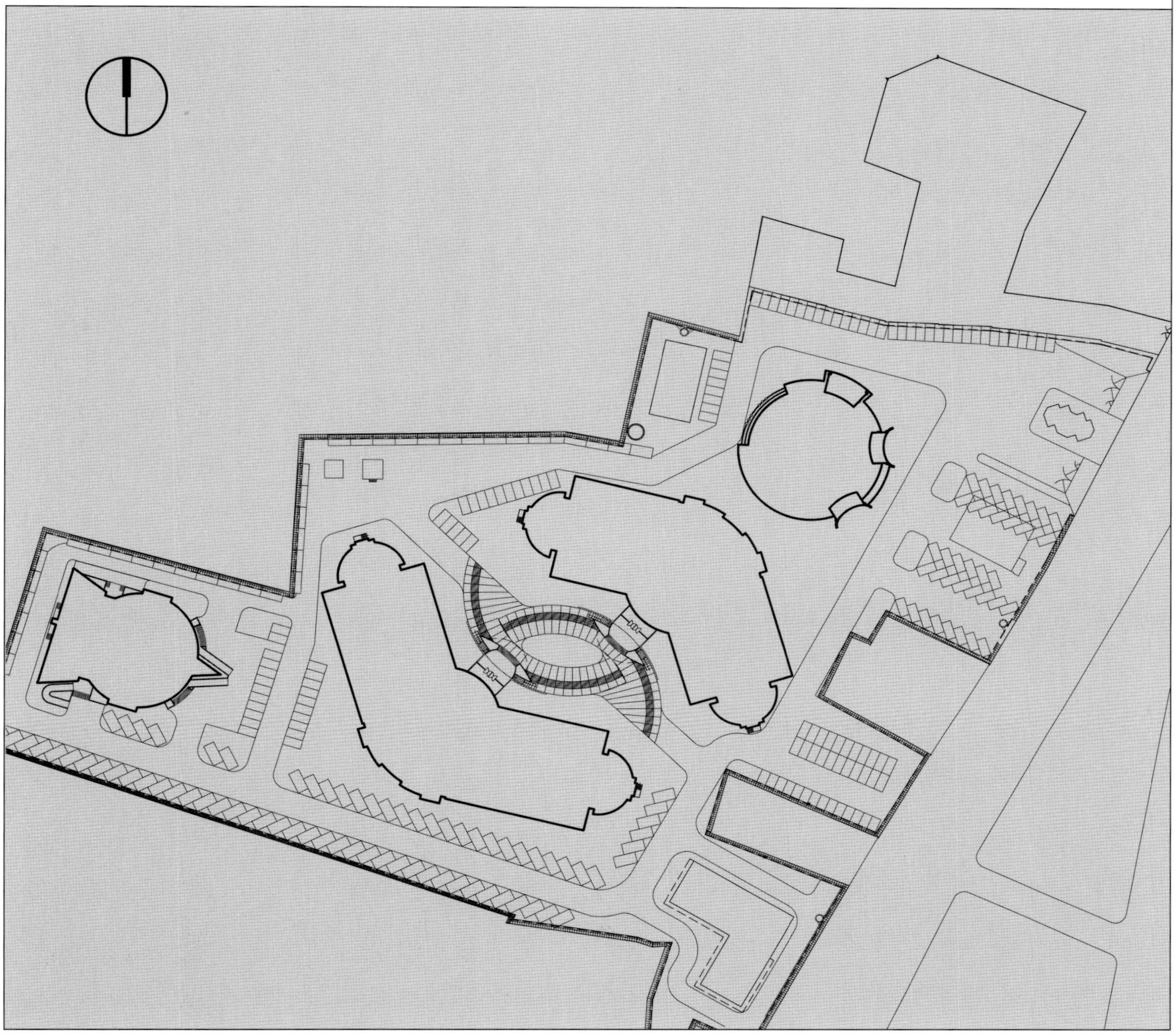

The site profile was a major constraint in the planning. Being an irregular shaped plot, it made zoning and creation of various axes challenging. The existing geometric alignment of approach roads dictated that the entrance be located to coincide with the originating point of the design axis and this was at the north-east corner of the plot. Equally challenging was the construction of this campus in a time period of as little as 11 months. An area of about 4,00,000 sft, fitted out with services, furniture and occupied in 11 months is a record of sorts in itself and an achievement of careful planning and methodical execution.

ebene

CLIENT
Business Parks of Mauritius Ltd

CATEGORY
Multi-tenanted Information Technology Park

LOCATION
Ebène, Mauritius

PRINCIPAL ARCHITECT
C N Raghavendran

DESIGN TEAM
Sumitra Ravindranath
Babu Varghese
V Ravi
K Chandrasekar
S Subbiah

CONTRACTORS
Larsen & Toubro and Shapoorji & Pallonji (Joint Venture)

STRUCTURAL, MECHANICAL & ELECTRICAL
Dallal Mott Mac Donald

LANDSCAPE ARCHITECTS
C R Narayana Rao Architects & Engineers

PROJECT DATE
2002 – 2004

1.02 EBENE CYBER TOWER

A landmark building, global in its outlook but with a local context, the Ebène Cyber Tower at Mauritius provides functional office spaces, supported by efficient utility and cutting-edge engineering services. It was designed to be the catalyst, the most preferred destination for businesses and professionals in Mauritius. Catering to about 10,000 professionals, this software hub is an inimitable combination of commercial, residential and enterprise infrastructure. Well-connected with the main city by a modern network of motorways and highways, the Cyber City is conveniently accessible from the main business and residential areas. The Ebène Cyber Tower is spread over 12 floors and is the largest built structure in Mauritius. The site area is about 150 acres. Relentless hard work was the force behind this famous Cyber City. In just 20 months, an area of 4,55,033 sft was custom-fitted with services, furniture, amenities and was handed over to the clients, ready for occupation by the businesses! A highly challenging feat, accomplished only by careful planning and methodical execution.

1.02 EBENE CYBER TOWER

Ebène received the Award for the Most Intelligent Building for the year 2005. This award is presented by a US 'Think Tank' Intelligent Community Forum (ICF). ICF presents awards each year from entries received from all over the world. At a function held on June 13 & 14 2005, New York, the jury selected Ebène Cyber Tower as its undisputed winner. The Ebène Cyber Tower distinguishes itself from all other buildings in the world through its world-class infrastructure, uncompromising security, hi-tech telecommunication, modern conference facilities and its strategic location. The cyber tower is also famous for its simple and functional design. The design of external elements were guided by not only aesthetic and climatic concerns but also by way of simplicity for construction and subsequently for maintenance. Almost all services were finished either with glazing or with aluminium composite panels, which require the least amount of effort from a maintenance standpoint. The double glazing uses high-performance glass with excellent thermal properties and provided high degree of insulation against heat and radiation increase. The design of the external elements was again guided by clean simple lines to form a visually appealing composition.

CONFERENCE
B

SITE PLAN

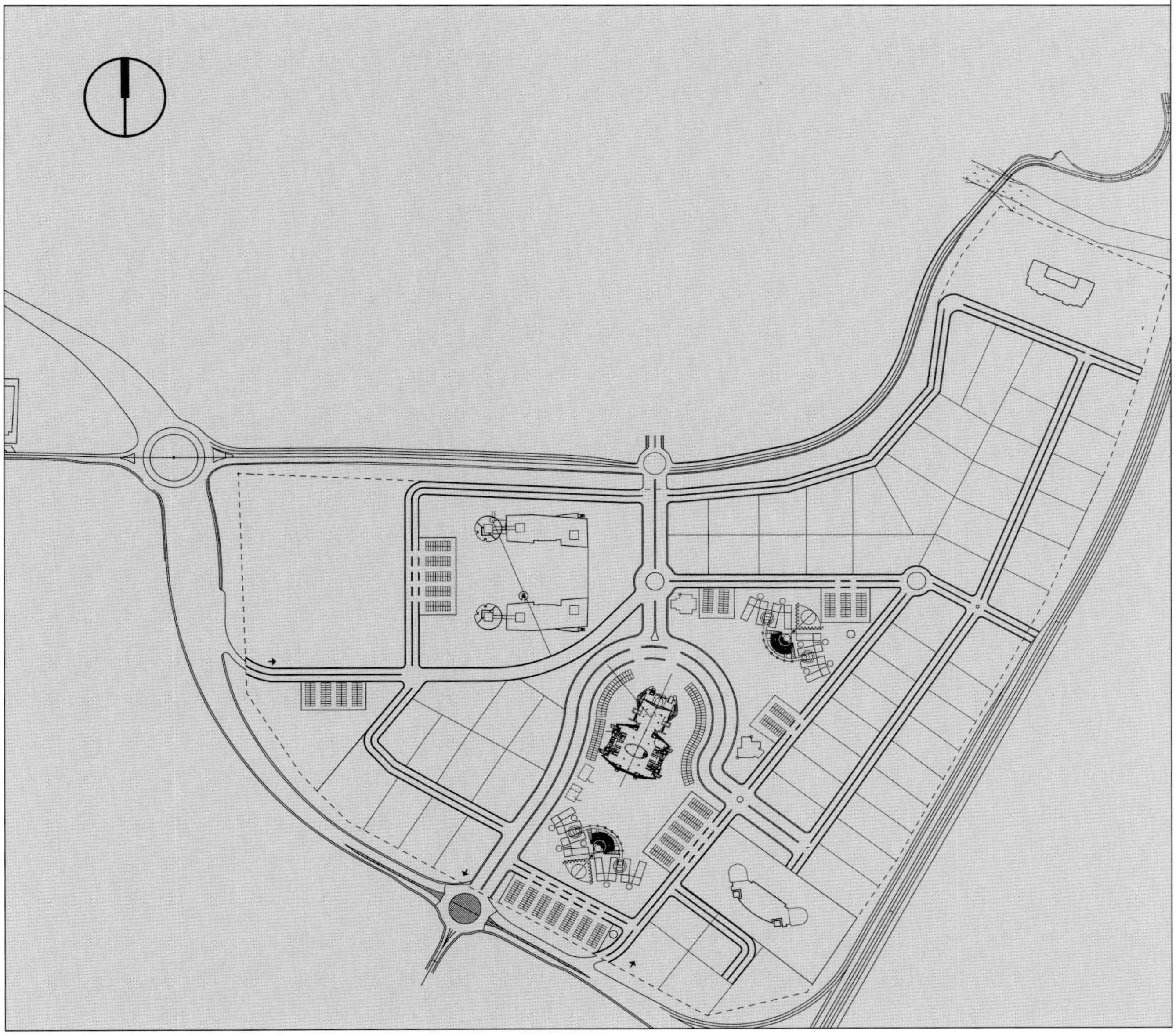

The site profile was a major constraint in the planning. Being an irregular shape, it made zoning and creation of various axes challenging. Equally challenging was the construction of this campus in a time period of 20 months. Flanked by landscaped green spaces, the tower was thoughtfully designed keeping the interests and activities of professionals in mind. The cyber tower is environmental-friendly, with the work spaces enhanced by bold and vibrant interior that beckons all the professionals from the island and from the world to come and work in this futuristic business centre.

FIRM NAME
Architect Hafeez Contractor

ADDRESS
29, Bank Street
Mumbai 400023
Maharashtra

CONTACT
Tel: +91 22 22661920
www.architecthafeezcontractor.com

No luck without hardwork... while pursuing architecture, Hafeez put this life mantra to test]

02 HAFEEZ CONTRACTOR

Born in 1950, Mumbai, Hafeez Contractor finished his schooling at the Town Boarding School, Nasik. As one of the most popular and talented student in his school, Hafeez used to find innovative and creative ways to deal with strict, old-fashioned matrons in the school. Recalling a school incident, he said, "One of our matrons was very strict and punished us if our shirt buttons were found missing. I designed a way out – whenever my button went missing, I carved one out of a chalk and stuck one on my shirt!" After finishing high school, Hafeez studied architecture at The Academy of Architecture in Mumbai while working in his cousin, Tehmasp Khareghat's architectural firm in the evenings. Here he honed his fundamental skills under the expert and patient guidance of his cousin, whom he also considers as his mentor. As a student of The Academy of Architecture, Hafeez won several design awards during 1970, 1974 and 1975. Upon graduating from The Academy of Architecture, Hafeez went on to pursue postgraduate studies in architecture from The Columbia University, New York. In 1982, with an office in a warehouse and three young men with similar vision and aspirations, Hafeez started his own practice. Today, more than two decades later, his office at Bank Street, Mumbai, is a bustling think tank of more than 300 employees. Hafeez's unique design approach has won him several accolades and prestigious projects. He is considered as one of the leading architects of India today. Provocative and unpredictable, Hafeez has achieved many milestones in a short time with his revolutionary ideas and his passion for perfection.

CLIENT
Infosys

CATEGORY
Software Development Block

LOCATION
Mysore, Karnataka

PRINCIPAL ARCHITECT
Hafeez Contractor

DESIGN TEAM
Anupam De
Rupa D'souza

CONTRACTORS
Sobha Developers

STRUCTURAL
Y S Sane Associates

HVAC
ARCO Consultant – Kavy Pradeep

LANDSCAPE ARCHITECTS
Masterplan – Shekhar James

PROJECT DATE
2004 – 2006

2.01 INFOSYS

Infosys, Mysore is regarded as the most employee-friendly work space in the IT industry today. Mr Narayan Murthy wanted Hafeez to create an avant-garde workspace for his IT professionals. Every new employee who becomes a part of the Infosys family, whether in India or abroad, has to cross the threshold of this software development block in Mysore to start his journey in Infosys. The building houses 2,500 professionals who undergo training before being absorbed by various Infosys offices, whether in India or abroad. The architect's inspiration was Origami, a Japanese art of folding paper; making a glass triangle the focal point of this structure. This 4,00,000 sft area has been made functional with innovative ideas & designs of structural engineers and a team of dedicated architects.

2.01 INFOSYS

Jagged façades and lopsided fragments style the aesthetics of the software development block. There are no concrete walls in this elevation. Laminated glass, double glazing and ceramic frit glass have been used to form the outer skin of this structure. Each elevation of this building projects a unique face. The staircases inside are steel, keeping with the image of the building. At night-time, the structure is lit up with artistic light formation and resembles a magnificent crystal. Unparalleled design and detailing has given this project a wide-spread national as well as international recognition.

SITE PLAN

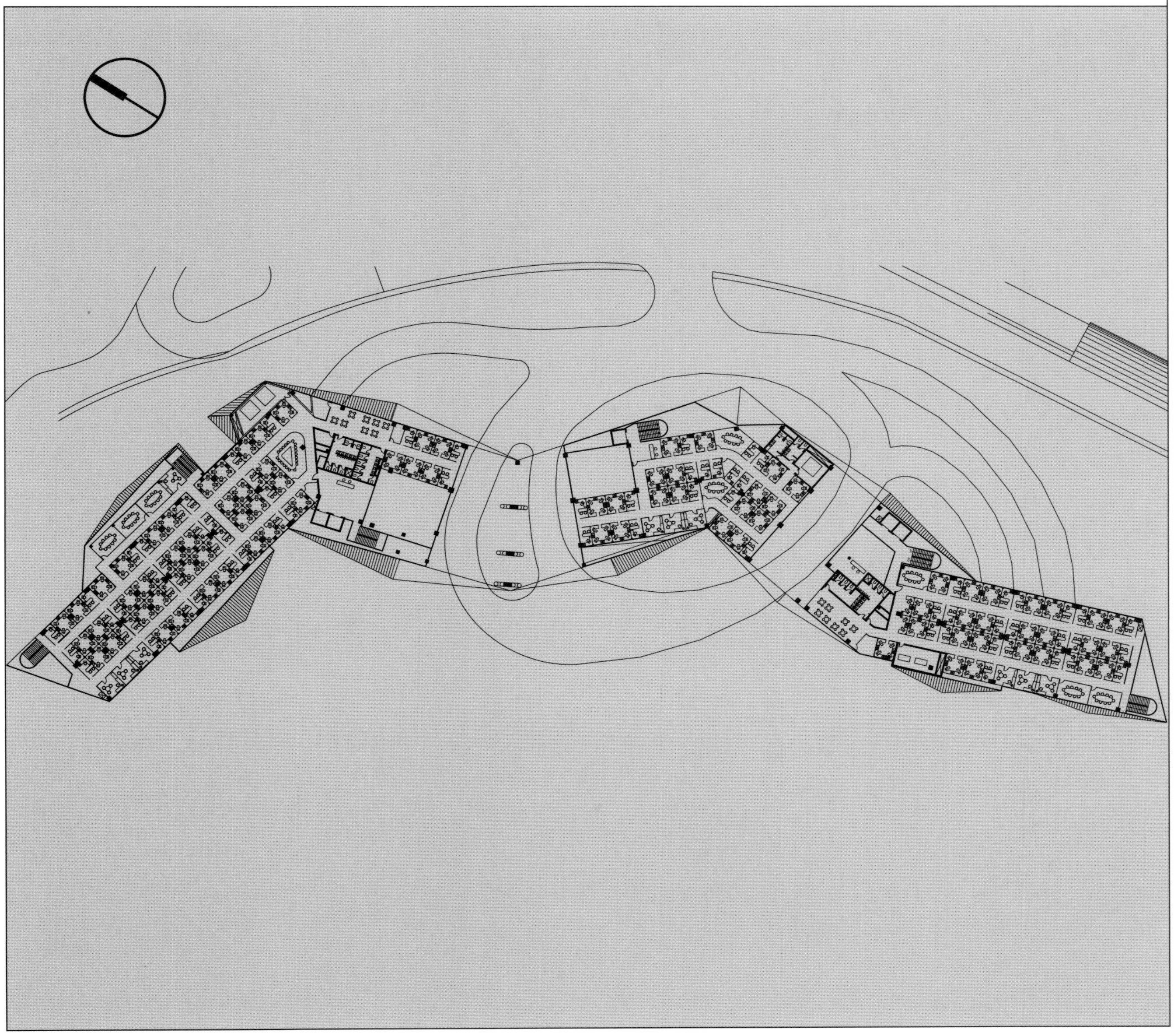

The typical open-plan interior layout has rectilinear profiles while featuring skewed atrium pockets on several edges. The extruding triangle, also referred to as the shell, is a primary member of the structure. The structure's glazing is done at this level. The glass is bound in place using secondary and tertiary framing support structures. The glass triangles are not merely aesthetic in nature; the space within them has been utilized to create additional rooms. In such complex elevations, the structural challenges were immense with the structural engineers playing a pivotal role.

CLIENT
Aditya Birla Group

CATEGORY
Corporate Office

LOCATION
Mumbai, Maharashtra

PRINCIPAL ARCHITECT
Hafeez Contractor

DESIGN TEAM
Anupam De

CONTRACTORS
M S Engineers, Mumbai

STRUCTURAL, HVAC
Sterling Engineering Consultancy Services

LANDSCAPE ARCHITECTS
Hafeez Contractor

PROJECT DATE
2002 – 2003

2.02 ADITYA BIRLA HQ

When the AV Birla Group, one of India's leading business houses, sought to establish their new corporate headquarters in the heart of Mumbai city, the Rhone Poulene House (R P House) set in Worli, Mumbai, seemed to provide the ideal setting. Hafeez's brief was simple – to remodel R P House, which would represent the strength and values of the A V Birla Group. This 4-storey structure houses four rectilinear blocks. Connecting structures were planned between the blocks to enable movement from one functional unit to the other. The brief also entailed inclusion of an additional parking area, a work area and the chairman's office. Hafeez took the bold decision of abandoning the obsolete expressions of the old structure and to create a contemporary aesthetic.

2.02 ADITYA BIRLA HQ

A new atrium, adorned by a glitzy chandelier, was added to connect the blocks leading up to the stairs and elevators. An additional floor designed in steel and glass to limit the load on the existing foundation was added to the structure. The glass is protected by a wing-like façade, topped with frosted glass. The metal wings of the façade dominate the exterior of the building. The entrance podium features a stainless steel sculpture representing A V Birla's brand equity across the globe. The lavishly landscaped podium houses the parking below it and functions as a private entry for top management. An exclusive entrance to the chairman's office features a glass bridge set over a water body.

SITE PLAN

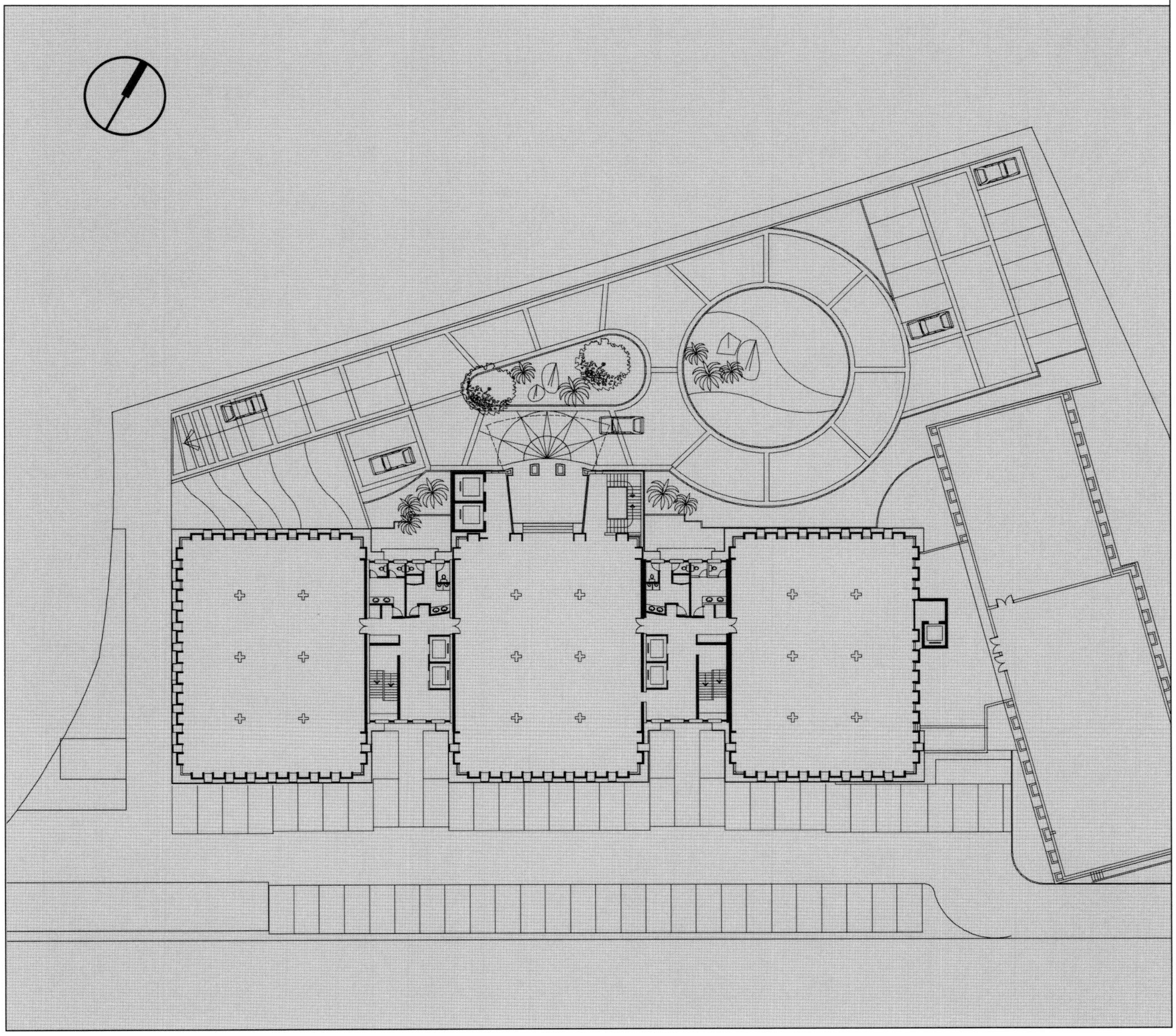

A major challenge was to break the preconceived notion that one has about retrofits and alterations made to existing buildings and the inherent hindrances they pose on the planning, and architecture. Hafeez's design succeeded in overcoming all such hindrances, thus presenting contemporary architecture that offers a sense of reverence to the past while projecting a bold, contemporary image befitting the company it represents. The end result is a structure that remains true to the Aditya Birla brand and resonates the brand's global presence.

FIRM NAME
Agrawal & Agrawal Architects

ADDRESS
96, Beltala Road
Near Bhawanipur
Kolkata
West Bengal

CONTACT
Tel: +91 33 24740570 / 73, +91 33 24763053
www.agrawalarchitects.com

One of the most important lesson while at college was that designing is a 'to and fro process', but what matters most is the correct beginning and the perfect finish]

03 J P AGRAWAL

J P Agrawal was born in Jhalod, Gujarat, in 1964. He completed his architecture from the Maharaja Sayaji Rao University, Vadodara. His first major breakthrough came with the design of first IT Park of West Bengal 'Infinity', which is widely appreciated and considered as a landmark in the state. According to J P, maximum use of natural elements can make the built space environment friendly. This thought always guides his company's projects. J P prides himself in being a conscientious architect. In the planning and execution stages of any project, he is very conscious about economic constraints and does not like to experiment at the cost of his clients' money. He believes that architecture is all about a complex solution addressed with common sense & scientific approach to achieve the end result, which is aesthetically pleasant & functional; and that modernity & nature should cohabit in harmony, for a building to function efficiently. J P's design process addresses every problem within the context, even at the cost of changing the design brief radically. His dream is to work on futuristic designs which can stand the test of time, sustaining the needs and dreams of the future generation.

CLIENT
Rahul Saraf

CATEGORY
IT Park

LOCATION
Kolkata, West Bengal

PRINCIPAL ARCHITECT
J P Agrawal

DESIGN TEAM
Arunava Maji
Palash Santra

CONTRACTORS
Aluwalia Contractors

STRUCTURAL & ELECTRICAL
S P A Consultants
Entask Electrics

HVAC
Air Treatment Engineering

LANDSCAPE ARCHITECTS
Design Accord

PROJECT DATE
2005 – 2006

3.01 TECHNOPOLIS

The brief was to design an IT Park with thoughtful and well-planned design considerations through systems, materials and amenities, which can qualify for LEED certification to prove environment friendly development. This was a challenge for a project having a very high FSI consumption. The project achieved targeted Gold Rating by conserving energy & natural resources, making it user-friendly, and providing healthy interiors with required level of oxygen. Moreover, the project was designed to ensure zero discharge to eliminate the wastage of water. Upon completion, Gold Rating was awarded to the project by US Green Building Council. The entire project was completed in a record period of 18 months despite several constrains and challenges.

3.01 TECHNOPOLIS

A distinctive feature of the project is the 40 ft high portico which acts as the drop-off and pick-up point for occupants. The 15,000 sft portico also acts as pedestrian plaza during break-off period due to its semi-covered ambiance with surrounding landscape flowing in continuity. Conceived as a steel structure supported on inclined steel pillars in tripod form, the support originates from a three feet high steel pedestal. The entire structure is designed to articulate the triangular pattern in the roof. The development of the portico structure raised two challenges. One was acquiring the high grade steel to strengthen the structure as the recommended steel was not manufactured in India. The second challenge was the availability of erection agency to execute the task within the significantly small time frame. The first was resolved using locally available steel while increasing the diameter of the pillars, since importing high grade steel was not a viable option. The second challenge added significantly more pressure since agencies were unwilling to commit to the time frame. Eventually the architects convinced the contractors to execute the structure with best of resources to meet the deadline.

LAYOUT PLAN

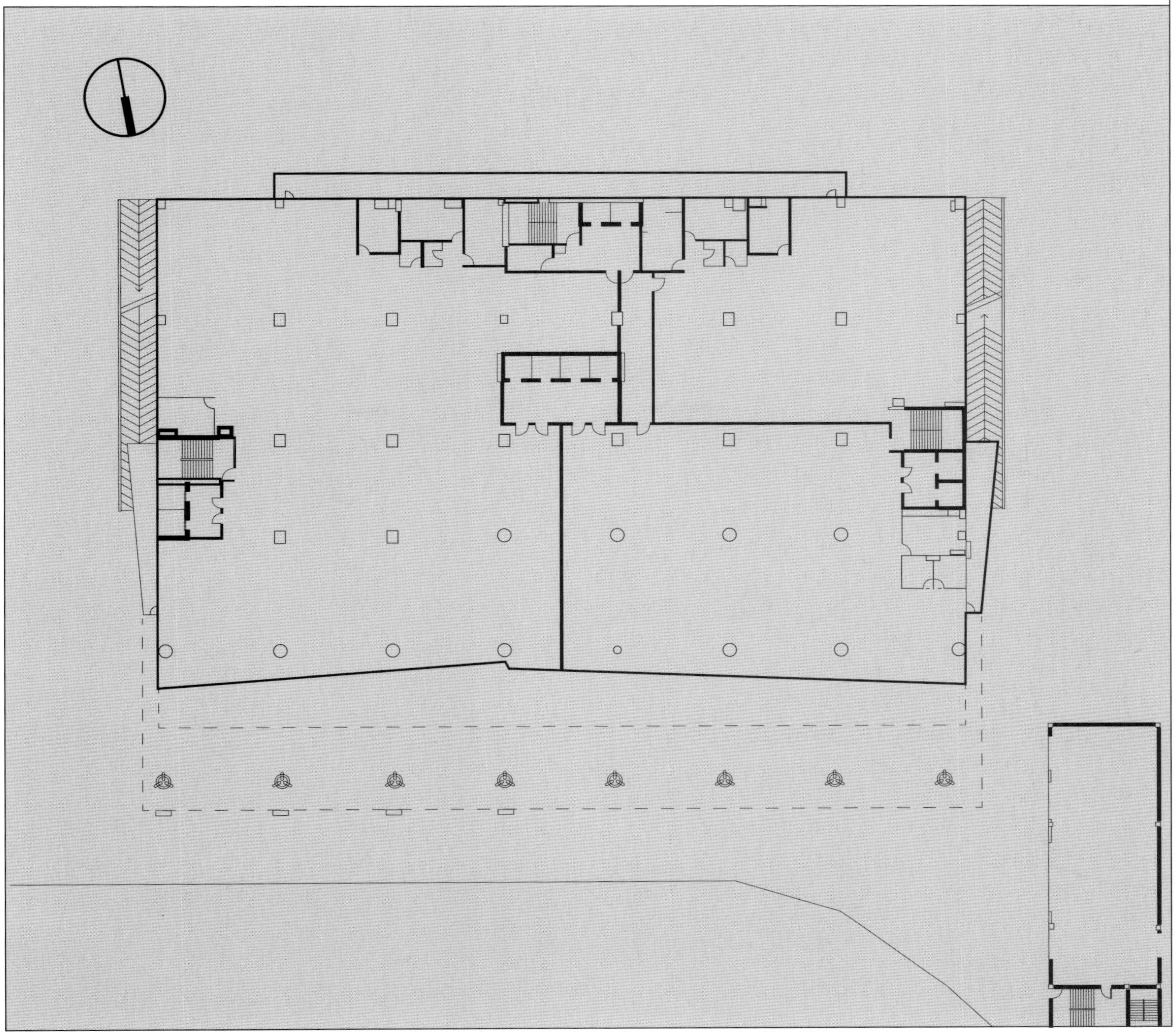

Special measures have been adopted to reduce the consumption of power. Overhangs with perforated metal sheets have been used, which discourage heat absorption thus reducing the cost of air-conditioning. The building is designed in such a way that the natural light is exploited to the maximum. All these considerations have helped the owners save at least Rs 3 per sft a month, which adds up to approximately Rs 2.5 crore a year! To ensure the savings of natural resources, the waste water is treated and recycled with the help of the a sewage treatment plant. The recycled water is used for the AC plant. The same water is also used for the garden and the fountains. Biodegradable waste is separated from nondegradable waste and the disposal takes place accordingly.

CITIBANK

CLIENT
Infinity Group

CATEGORY
IT Park

LOCATION
Kolkata, West Bengal

PRINCIPAL ARCHITECT
J P Agrawal

DESIGN TEAM
K Dasgupta

CONTRACTORS
Sunsam Properties

STRUCTURAL, MECHANICAL & ELECTRICAL
T K Hazra
T K Mukherjee

HVAC
D P Saha

LANDSCAPE ARCHITECTS
Agrawal & Agrawal Architects

PROJECT DATE
1997 – 2007

3.02 INFINITY

Infinity, is the first IT park in West Bengal to have won several accolades for its architectural excellence. J P's contributions and efforts were also appreciated in a book discussing the 50 young achievers of Kolkata. The clients, wanted the development to be highly sophisticated and yet close to nature. The design concept has addressed this philosophy. The project started in 1996 and was planned to be completed in two phases. Out of the total area of 3,500,000 sft, the development of Phase I was 1,10,000 sft. The design comprises of two towers connected with an atrium and three courtyards. The entire concept was based on the central idea to achieve a sense of openness and connectedness with the natural environment.

3.02 INFINITY

The IT Park has been designed to be a place where the employees can come with their friends and family and showcase their place of work with a sense of pride. The planning incorporates many interactive points in the common areas, a well-stocked cafeteria with the best facilities that the industry can offer. Special attention was given to employee comfort, such as controlled lighting, glare-free natural light, huge terrace area, greenery in abundance and an environment which is natural yet sophisticated. The strength of the design is communicated through the bold statement of the building form. This is further enhanced with the reflections of the triangular space frames and the mirrored glasses creating drama and illusion of a square courtyard within the building form. Play of double height areas and terraces at different levels, gives an impression of a campus rather than an office building. A cafeteria in the middle of the atrium becomes a hang out place for the employees in the evenings.

INFINITY

IN Y

LAYOUT PLAN

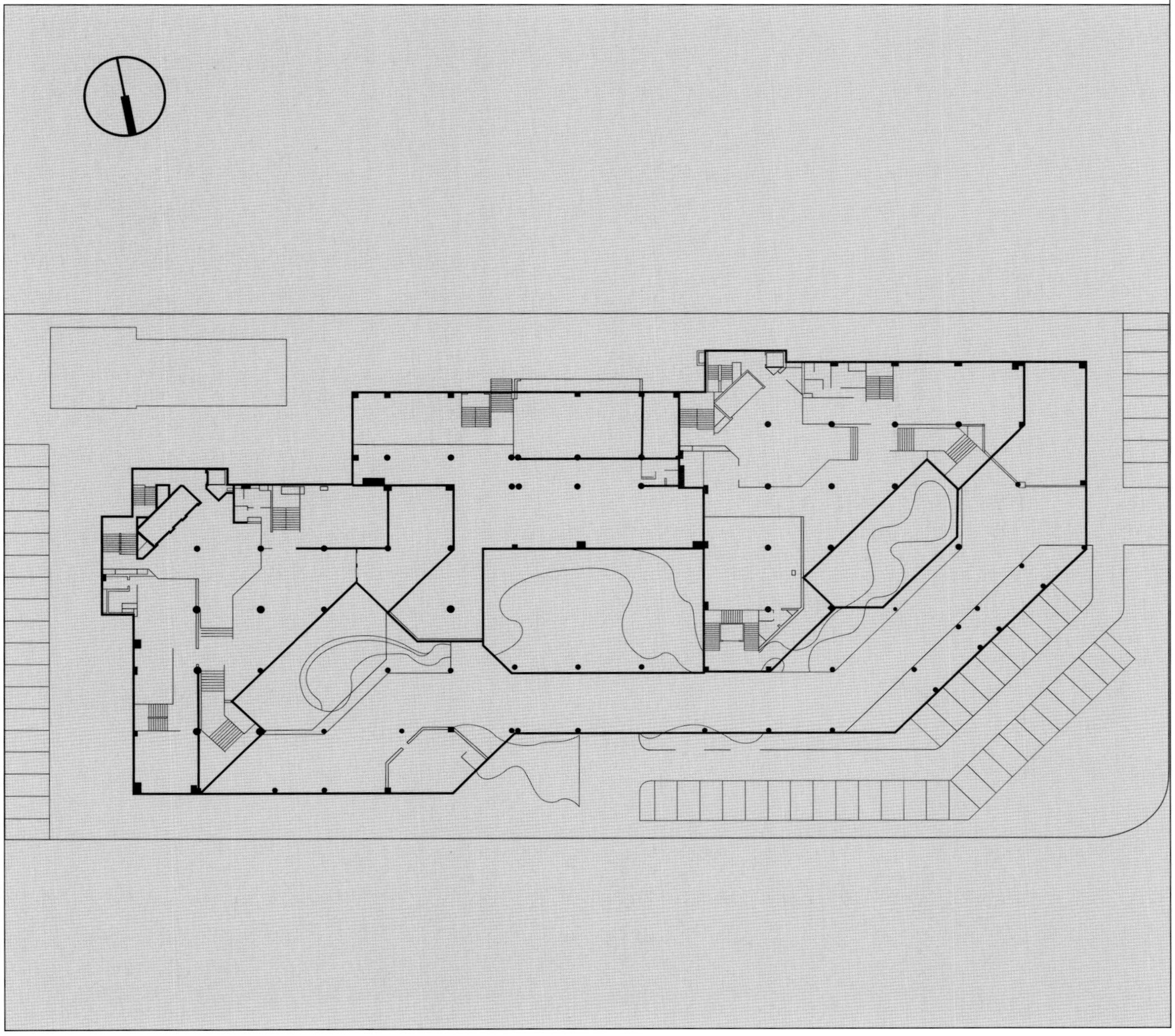

During the site planning phase, the challenge was the viability of a driveway, which was planned along the entire length of the site connecting the three courtyards. Given the soil condition, a pile foundation was required for the driveway, which had a cost impact the client was unwilling to accept. However, the architect was convinced about the portico structure being a key element in the design and was not willing to compromise on the same. The specifications were modified elsewhere to save on costs without compromising on the overall quality and the end product resulted in a design that satisfied the client with a unique ambience.

FIRM NAME
Malik Architecture Ecology Spirit

ADDRESS
Kaiser-I-Hind
1/6 Currimbhoy Road
Ballard Estate
Mumbai 400038
Maharashtra

CONTACT
Tel: +91 22 22642170
www.malikarchitecture.com

Architecture is not about buildings. It is about the environment. It is a summation of all arts and about understanding the evolving social fabric]

04 KAMAL S MALIK

Kamal S Malik was born in Shimla, Himachal Pradesh, in 1949. His love for nature drew him to architecture, which he believed would give him an opportunity to pursue his interest in nature and environment. He studied in SPA, Delhi under the innovative guidance of Professor Bruno D'Souza. He believes that architecture is a social science and one should rely on intuition as opposed to education for architectural direction. Malik Architecture was established to explore the diktat of architecture as ecology and spirit, an endeavour towards the movement of a contemporary expression in design for the sub-continent. Kamal's work approach caters to the unique needs of every project as he carefully evaluates sun angles, the available local materials and the sociological factors. The result is completely diverse, relevant and contextual solutions. Kamal has received many awards for his work. Articles praising his designs have been published in both Indian and International magazines. About his chosen profession, he says, "I love the creative aspect of my profession as well as the opportunity to be a part of constantly changing and evolving environment and above all, to be continuously amazed at the rich heritage and past whilst probing the future".

LUPIN
RESEARCH PARK

CLIENT
Lupin Research Park

CATEGORY
R & D Centre

LOCATION
Pune, Maharashtra

PRINCIPAL ARCHITECT
Kamal S Malik

DESIGN TEAM
K Chaudhary
M Tipnis
R Parmar

CONTRACTORS
R L Dalal

STRUCTURAL, MECHANICAL & ELECTRICAL
Sterling Consultancy – Vikas Joshi

HVAC
J G Gharat, Kamal S Malik

LANDSCAPE ARCHITECTS
Kamal S Malik

PROJECT DATE
2000 – 2001

4.01 LUPIN RESEARCH PARK

The act of research and discovery is essentially an intuitive function. This complex therefore explores those elements that foster and inspire intuitive thought, which is the core of the creative process. The inspiration for the complex is the timeless *mandala*, with the administration complex representing the head at the highest point of the hill and the main research park flowing south to north, wrapped around a central courtyard. At a first glance, the structure is reminiscent of and echoes the timelessness of an ancient habitat or a human settlement. Portrayed as a rocky out-crop at the base of the hill, it disguises itself as clay masses juxtaposed, emanating from and merging into the hill. As one approaches closer, this cluster of terracotta massing gives way to a more orderly and identifiable form as is represented by the single long wall that stems from the hill and flows downwards. Punctuated by intriguing functional masses and the amphitheatre, the recessed courtyard of the formulation labs and the gush of water from an overhead channel, the wall develops a huge puncture that is the entrance to the main complex. Sensitive use of colour and the play of light and shade add to the strength of the composition.

LUPIN

4.01 LUPIN RESEARCH PARK

The entrance court is dramatic. A huge water fall on the northern flank and a tilted aluminium cube (the auditorium) nestled against the hill frame, a series of juxtaposed walls splicing into each other. The entrance foyer looks up at the hill and down to the central café / library on one side and the courtyard on the other thereby, generating a powerful south-north axis that forms the mainstay of movement within the complex. Light and shadow, like day and night, are intertwined. It is these two elements that have been juxtaposed in a myriad number of permutations to produce a rhapsody; from the ethereal play of light on the walls, ramp and steps leading to the animal house; the surrealistic imposition of the pergolas sociography onto the floor, the silver prism of the auditorium and the dark silhouette of the cube sculpture; the splintering of light from tiny points to lengthening stippled bands moving like a sun-dial, the dappled play of light and shade in the main library / dining court; the gradual increase of light intensity as one moves up the north-south axis echoing the very act of regeneration / re-birth; all representative of the dialogue and rapport that the built forms have with the sun.

SITE PLAN

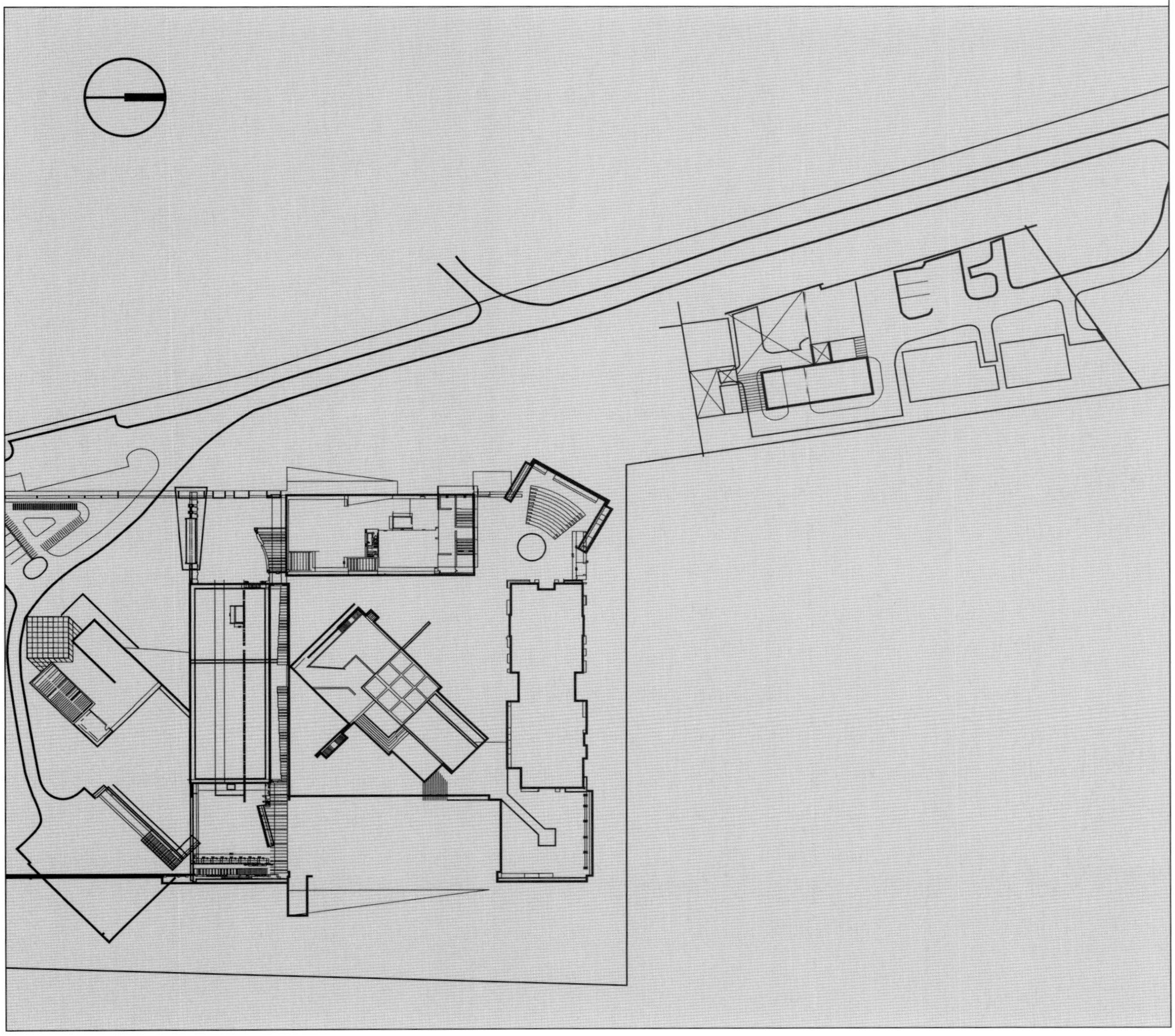

Major openings are in the north and east and layer solid masses on the south and west. The main entrance court has two interesting water bodies; the first, a 50 ft long transparent sheet of water flowing both sides of the entrance court and punctuated by a smaller water gargoyle and the second being a two-level stepped pool from which rises the sculptured mass of the aluminium cube that is the auditorium. By far the most fascinating water body is the *kund*. An enormous sheet of water, on which floats the vault of the dining space, accessed on one face as a dramatic flight of steps and on the other by the verdant green of the lawn. The main north-south axis culminates in the hill vista and the auditorium foyer on the one end and the integrated common facilities complex and valley on the other. The library, fitness centre and dining areas are an integral part of the main pergola covered court that opens out into a huge garden and views of the valley on one side, the amphitheatre on another and a sharp bank of terraced steps leading to the hill on the third.

CLIENT
Institute of Oncological Sciences

CATEGORY
Hospital

LOCATION
Jaipur, Rajasthan

PRINCIPAL ARCHITECT
Kamal S Malik

DESIGN TEAM
K Chaudhary

CONTRACTORS
Ahluwalia Contracts (I) Ltd

STRUCTURAL
Sterling Engg & Consultancy Services Pvt Ltd
Vikas Josh & Associates

LANDSCAPE ARCHITECTS
Raju Pradhan

PROJECT DATE
1997 – 2003

4.02 INSTITUTE OF ONCOLOGICAL SCIENCES

The Institute of Oncological Sciences was intended to be an island of excellence, providing a comprehensive cancer cover for the entire state of Rajasthan. Malik recognized that this was a unique opportunity to weave together two seemingly paradoxical streams: the philosophy of the east with the technical excellence of the west. In a bid to address the mental health of the patient in addition to the physical, Malik relied on his unique understanding of the timeless philosophy expounded by the architectural wizards of primordial India. The planning process revolved around creating a patient-friendly environment, one that would make them feel comfortable and at home. This vision is evident in the emphasis given to functionality. Circulation routes for staff, patients and visitors were meticulously designed and segregated to boost convenience. The diverse departments branch out from a central spine and are placed strategically based on function. The Institute captures the spirit of Jaipur's heritage. The exterior echoes a timeless association with its surroundings through the interplay of huge stone walls and intersecting plans, complex geometry, traditional red and beige desert sandstones, textured and seamlessly combined into the overall composition and the play of light as it changes direction with each passing minute.

4.02 INSTITUTE OF ONCOLOGICAL SCIENCES

Since nearly 70 percent of cancer therapies are conducted on an outpatient basis, the specifications for this division were detailed as a two-level zone, comprising a Diagnostics Centre and a Therapy Centre. To conserve energy as well as optimise area usage, the plan provides for facilities that enable cutting off power to specific departments when not in use without affecting the other departments. The design effectively provides for the induction of cutting-edge medical equipment and IT systems without compromising on the local flavour of the design. The outer shell of the configuration and the inner spaces clearly find their inspiration in their locale. The main OPD is designed as a *chaurasta* with radiating streets leading out to all out-patient diagnostic and therapy activities. Multiple courtyard spaces that gently filter suffused light into the circulation and waiting areas have been created. Light is drawn through a fascinating array of skylights into the multiple out-patient courts from the ribbon of light that pours through the observatory-like dome to the sixteen sculptured skylights of the main OPD.

SITE PLAN

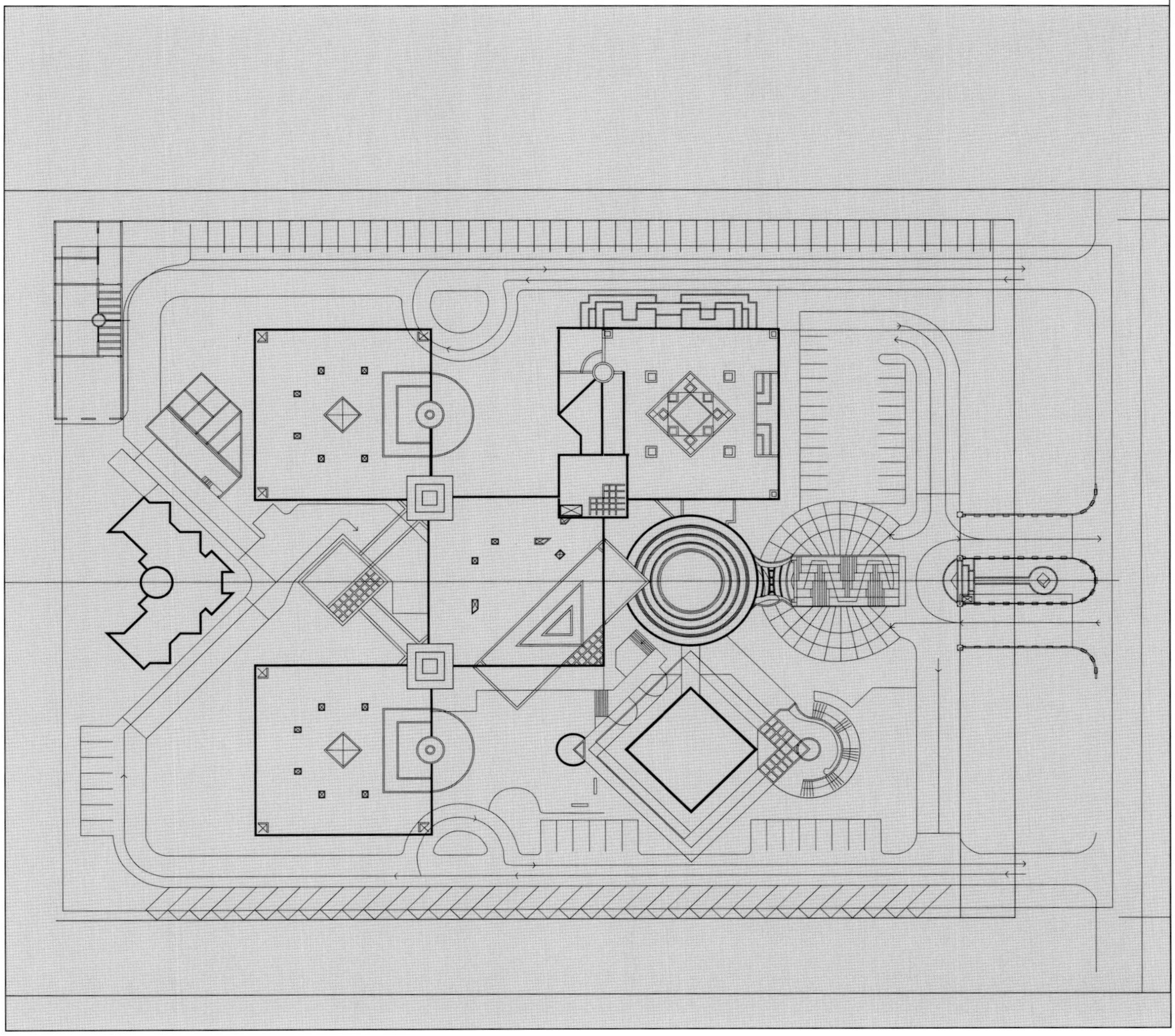

The plan draws upon the concept of the *mandala*, the very model for the city of Jaipur itself. It follows the principle of nine squares with main blocks consisting of an OPD, a diagnostics centre, an administration wing, OT Suites / ICU, in-patient and garden courts with meditation cells. The spine runs diagonally across the *mandala,* connecting all the major activities. The harsh extremes of the Rajasthan climate necessitated the study of sun directions, consequent placement of fenestration to ensure that they were in deep shade, thick stone walls for insulation and the creation of semi-open landscaped courts that would permit both, visitors and patients to enjoy the outdoors. Recognizing the end user to be vernacular, perhaps even illiterate, the architect used a truly innovative way of facilitating visitor movement. The problem of language / signage systems was completely solved when the architect used the passion for colour that is the hallmark of Rajasthan into simple colour-coded pathways. The traditional *chaurasta* of radiating streets, coupled with colour-coding, resolved and made the process of path-finding effortless.

FIRM NAME
Karan Grover & Associates

ADDRESS
Kirti Tower
Tilak Road
Vadodara 390001
Gujarat

CONTACT
Tel: +91 265 2427522 / 44

My designs reflect my passion for heritage and landscapes.
I design for Indians]

05 KARAN GROVER

Karan Grover was born in Mumbai. He completed his education from Mayo College, Ajmer and was a national-level swimmer. The call of architecture was so strong that Karan Grover decided to focus his attention towards fulfilling his dreams instead of joining his father's business. After completing undergraduate studies at the Vadodara School of Architecture of the Maharaja Sayajirao University, he pursued his postgraduate studies from the Architectural Association, London. In 1975, he floated a partnership, Patel & Grover Associates, with a friend and confidant Mr Manoj Patel. After a 10-year strong partnership, they went their separate ways. Karan Grover is now the proud owner of Karan Grover & Associates. Karan has won several awards and accolades. In 2004, he won the LEED Award for the first platinum building for CII Godrej Green Business Centre, Hyderabad. He also won the nomination for Champaner, a fourteenth-century city. It was India's nomination to UNESCO for World Heritage Status in 2004. He is working towards emphasizing the importance of green and sustainable architecture among students and fellow architects. He thinks it is a worthy and important cause, which everyone should contribute to and make this planet a better place to work and live in.

CLIENT
Confederation of Indian Industry

CATEGORY
Institutional

LOCATION
Hyderabad, Andhra Pradesh

PRINCIPAL ARCHITECT
Karan Grover

DESIGN TEAM
P A Pithawala
S Parmar

CONTRACTORS
Consolidated Construction Consortium Ltd

BUILDING SIMULATION
T E R I

STRUCTURAL, MECHANICAL & ELECTRICAL
Comten Engineers
Spectral Services Consultants

HVAC
Spectral Services Consultants

LANDSCAPE ARCHITECTS
Aarti Chari, Shaheer Associates

PROJECT DATE
2001 – 2004

5.01 CII SOHRABJI GBC

The Confederation of Indian Industry (CII) – Sohrabji Godrej Green Business Centre is the "Centre of Excellence" of the Confederation of Indian Industry for energy efficiency, green buildings, renewable energy, water, environment & recycling and climate change activities in India. The Centre is a joint initiative of the Government of Andhra Pradesh, Confederation of Indian Industry (CII) and the House of Godrej with the technical support of USAID – a unique model of a successful public-private partnership. Karan Grover & Associates were called in as project architects as they were already involved in designing the Centre of Excellence in Bengaluru for CII. After a design tour that spanned the length and breadth of USA, Karan and his team returned home disappointed. His extensive research indicated that no building, which promoted green was actually green in its creation. Superimposing a blue print that was essentially developed for the US commercial market on Indian conditions represented its own unique set of problems.

5.01 CII SOHRABJI GBC

The building is centred around a circular courtyard, with a series of small courtyards in between. The circular form of the building minimizes the surface area of the walls exposed to the heat. The screen wall or *jaali* is effectively used to cut down on harsh sunlight, yet allow the flow of wind. The use of a wind tower is one of the traditional passive-cooling techniques of the sub-continent. Here, it has been combined with the HVAC system such that there is a decrease in energy consumption. The air that goes into the Air Handling Unit (AHU) is precooled by the wind tower, reducing the air temperature by 3°C to 5°C. Thus, reducing the load on the AHU. The wind tower itself is made of hollow masonry and acts as a 'thermal mass'. It is cooled periodically by trickling water from the top, and the air passing through loses heat. The building's innovative design won the LEED rating points for innovation and design. Arranged in a circular plan broken by a series of courtyards, a main central courtyard and four smaller ones on the side, the building is distinctive and classy. The idea is to connect with the outside world which helps you rejuvenate and perform better. The Technology Centre features partly slanting double glazed, argon filled glass panels which provide 75 percent light but transmit only 25 percent of the heat from the sunlight.

SITE PLAN

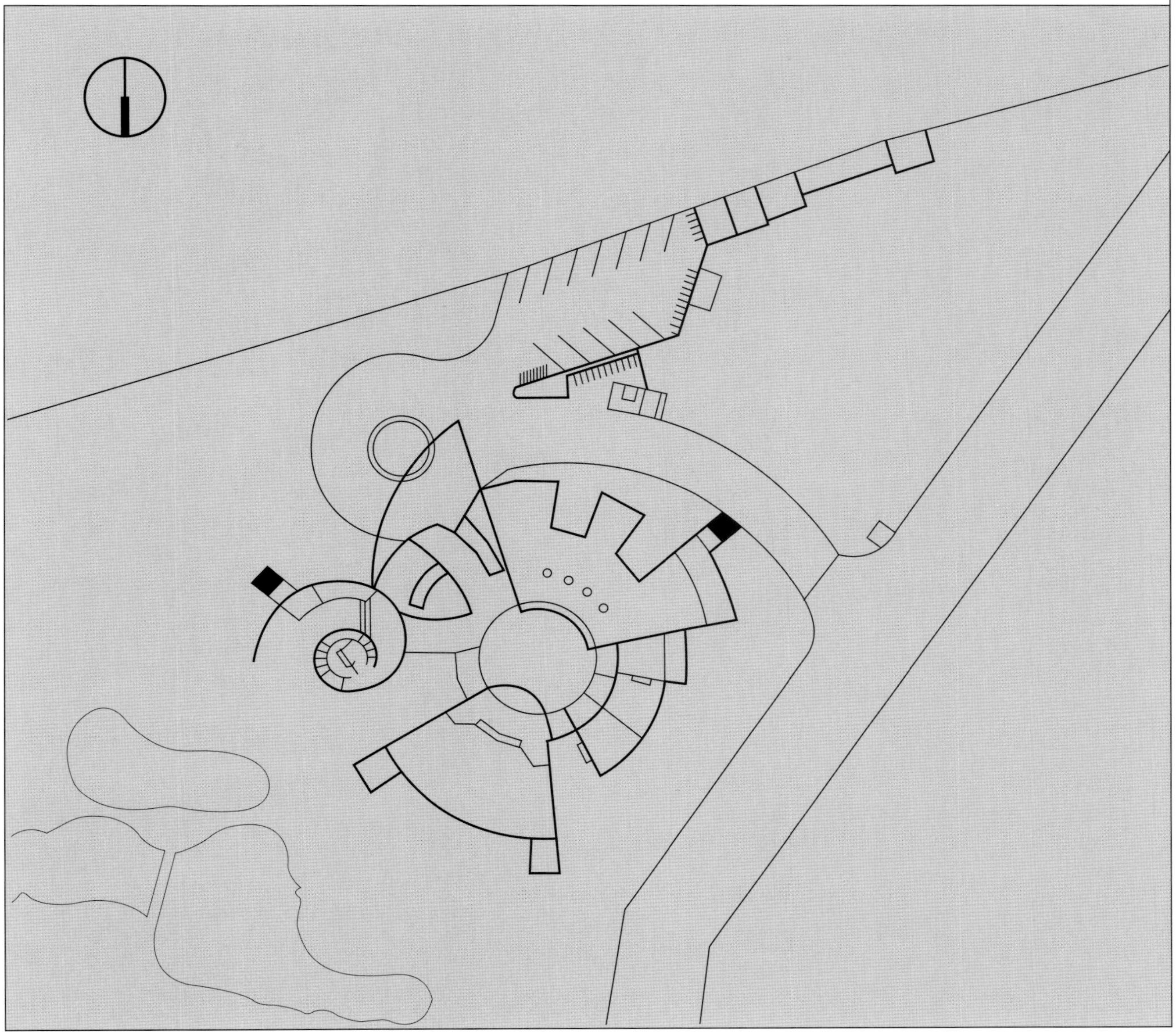

The biggest challenge with this particular construction was that the idea of sustainable design is completely inter-linked. It is an outcome of team deliberations and team spirit as opposed to the work of an individual. All consultants jointly addressed sustainable issues, where each discipline compliments and reinforces the other. A case in point was that of landscaping. When Karan Grover drew up a 2-acre expanse of lawn on the 5-acre plot, he was asked by the landscape consultant to specify the grass he envisioned. When that decision was taken, the water management consultant computed the water requirement. The same was validated by the commissioning agents who then computed the output of the pump required to meet the said water requirement. A local architect gave an estimate for the installation of the pump. Finally, based on variables including budgeting constraints, it was decided that 7,000 sft would be the optimum size for the lawn. This particular example is just one of the many examples that drove home the fact that no single decision was a stand-alone decision but an integrated one.

CLIENT
Confederation of Indian Industry

CATEGORY
Institutional

LOCATION
Bengaluru, Karnataka

PRINCIPAL ARCHITECT
Karan Grover

DESIGN TEAM
P A Pithawala
H Parmar

ENVIRONMENTAL DESIGN
Brian Ford & Associates

CONTRACTORS
Shapoorji Pallonji Engineering Ltd

STRUCTURAL, MECHANICAL & ELECTRICAL
Cruthi Consultants
Spectral Services Consultants

HVAC
Spectral Services Consultants

LANDSCAPE ARCHITECTS
Shaheer Associates

PROJECT DATE
2000 – 2001

5.02 CII ABB INSTITUTE

The Confederation of Indian Industry (CII) wanted to establish four Centres of Excellence in India. A 21,000 sft plot in Bengaluru overlooking the Nandi Hills was selected for this endeavour. Karan Grover wanted to add an element of surprise to this project. He wanted the building to be hidden from a distance so that when the visitors arrive at this destination, they are surprised to see this magnificent structure. Therefore, from a distance, only the four wind towers are visible, the building is below the road and surprises you as you arrive at this site. This institute of quality was awarded the Indian Institute of Architects (IIA) – Snowcem Award for the outstanding Public Building of the year in 1997.

5.02 CII ABB INSTITUTE

The wind towers cool the ambient air by 11°C, so there is no air conditioning used in this building. This building is cooled passively. Other elements have been inspired from the homes of yore and given a modern interpretation. Vibrant colours adorn the building such as yellow and *kesari* giving this structure an authentic yet modern appearance. Two significant lessons were learnt from this project. The first was that the architect must be an integral part of the team in the site selection process as his inputs can have enormous ramifications to the approach and setting of the building. In this specific case, access to the structure was at a lower level of the site. Consequently, while approaching the structure, the first visible sight would be that of the parking lot. Instead, the architects chose an approach road from a nearby hill top and were instrumental in acquiring the additional land from the State Government. Consequently, as one drives up to the main courtyard, one is greeted with an extraordinary view of the surrounding Nandi Hills.

LAYOUT PLAN

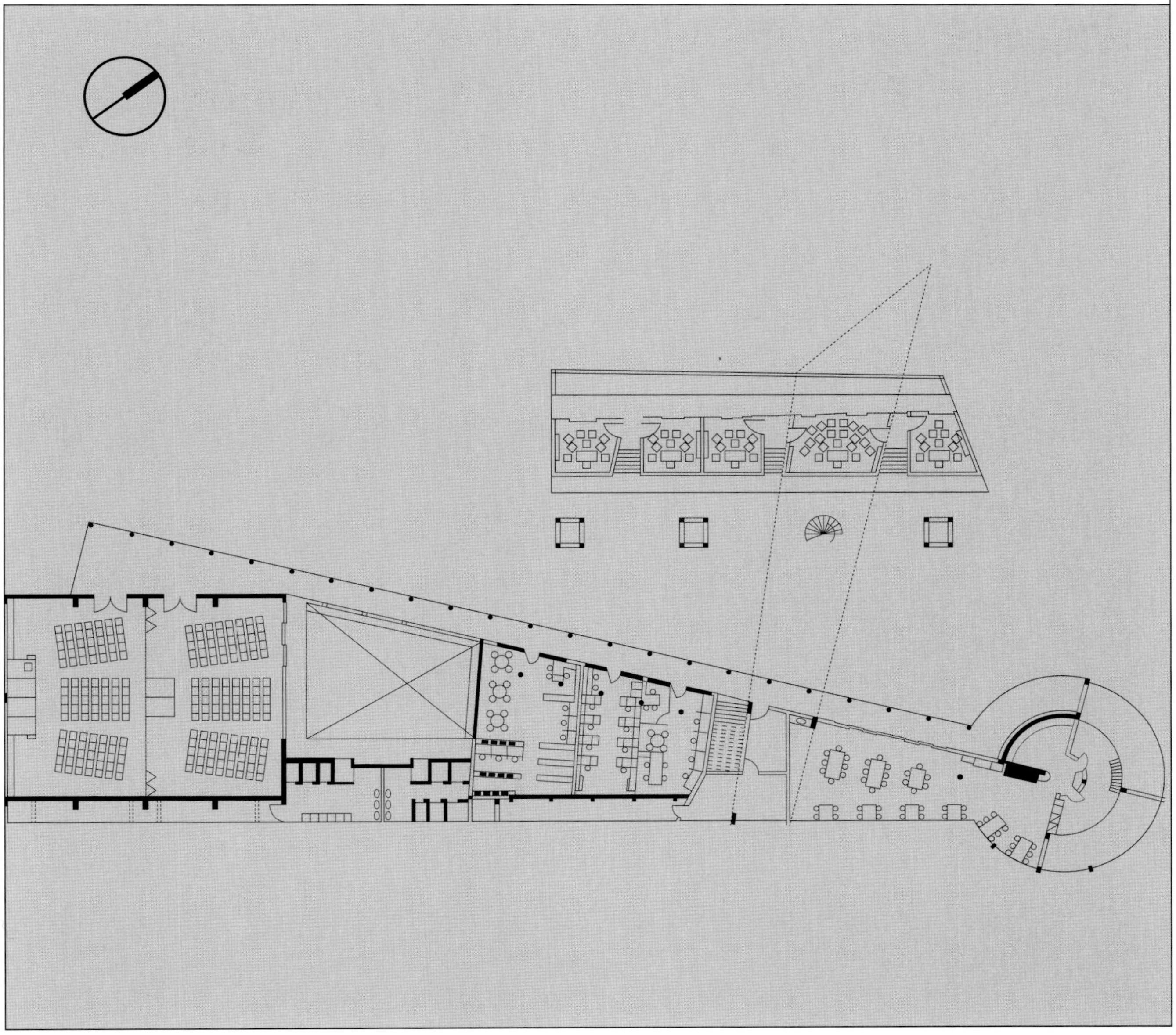

The project integrates time-tested architectural traditions, with a little bit of reinterpretation into mainstream contemporary architecture. The reinterpretation of the traditional concept of wind towers as passive cooling devices has been a major architectural feature in this project not just functionally but also aesthetically as the four iconic towers mark the formidable presence of the institute.

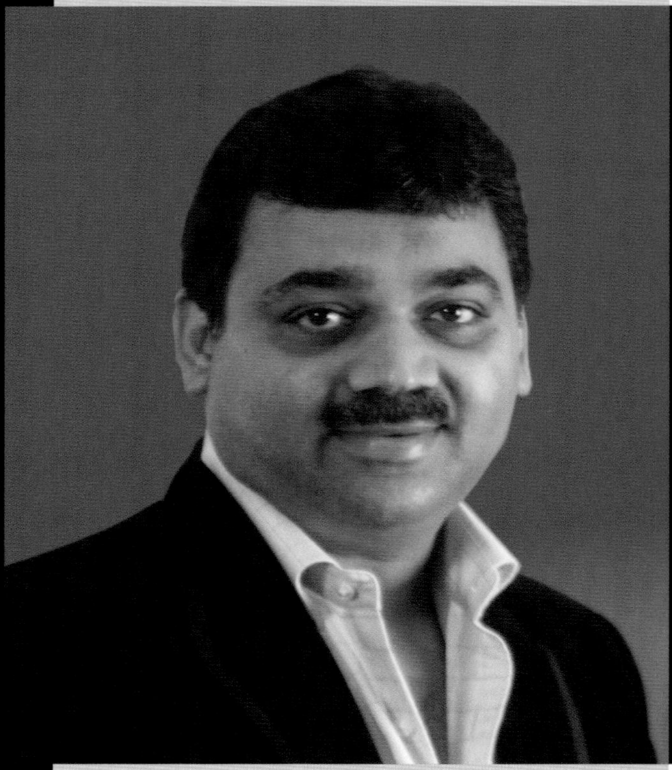

FIRM NAME
Nimish Choksi Architects

ADDRESS
Ground Floor, Arvind Niwas
Near Flyover, Athwa Gate
Surat 395001
Gujarat

CONTACT
Tel: +91 261 2470248

Nimish Choksi subscribes to the mantra 'God is in the detail' and is committed to the belief that 'quality supercedes quantity']

06 NIMISH CHOKSI

Nimish Choksi was born in Surat in 1967. He completed his high school education from the Lourdes Convent School, Surat and pursued his junior college education from St Xavier's. After graduating from the Institute of Environmental Design (IED), Vidya Nagar, Nimish Choksi went to Malaysia to work with Mr Ken Yeang, a renowned architect who advocates the concept of tropical high-rise building. Here Nimish Choksi was exposed to the idea that the energy devouring glass box high rise of the west cannot be the solution for developing countries with tropical climate. "Ken Yeang's design for the tropical high-rise inspired me and I decided to work in his office and make his work the basis of my thesis." Working with Ken was a life changing experience for Nimish Choksi.

CLIENT
Babulal Sanghvi Residence

CATEGORY
Luxury Private Residence

LOCATION
Surat, Gujarat

PRINCIPAL ARCHITECT
Nimish Choksi

DESIGN TEAM
Vaishali Choksi
Kekul Mistry

STRUCTURAL, MECHANICAL & ELECTRICAL
Bimal Jariwala

CONTRACTORS
Rivaa Constructions

HVAC
Jay Air Systems

LANDSCAPE
Varghese (Bengaluru)

PROJECT DATE
2004 – 2006

6.01 BABULAL SANGHVI RESIDENCE

The lavish 32,291 sft plot was to house a home – contemporary in appeal, Indian in function and impeccable in finish. The spatial planning of the house was conceived in such a manner that a perfect synergy emerged between the architecture and interior design of the house on its completion. The house was planned keeping in mind the minutest detail of interior spaces. In spite of the house being located in a populated part of the city, it was designed to be a private haven in harmony with the outdoors. The house has three levels – lower ground floor, ground floor and the first floor. The lower ground floor is designed as a recreational area, housing a 1,000 sft state-of-the-art home-theatre, fully equipped gymnasium and a mini spa with children's pool, family jacuzzi, steam and sauna facilities. The ground floor is designed as a social area, housing the living room, the formal and private dining room, family room, guest room and the children activity room. The first floor is designed as the private area with a master bedroom, four other bedrooms, a common lounge with library and the *pooja* room.

6.01 BABULAL SANGHVI RESIDENCE

Public rooms in the house such as the living room open to the private and formal garden, while the guest and the family rooms open to cosy private outdoors. The heart of the house is in fact the atrium which connects the ground floor and the first floor and creates a degree of fluidity between the interior and exteriors through its unique skylight roof. The house is centrally air-conditioned with a total capacity of 80 TR, designed in such a way that any room can be individually cooled as required. All windows are double-glazed and slide into specially designed hollow double walls creating a seamless connection with the outdoors. Sliding louvred wooden doors, which also retract into the hollow walls, are cleverly designed in place of the usual iron grills used for security. 20 mm thick Sicilia marble of the highest quality was specially imported from Italy for the flooring of the house. The serene landscaping all around the house helps to create a quiet oasis shielded from the urban chaos creating a dream house in the heart of the city and providing a home to three generations of a family living in peaceful harmony.

Optoma

GROUND FLOOR PLAN

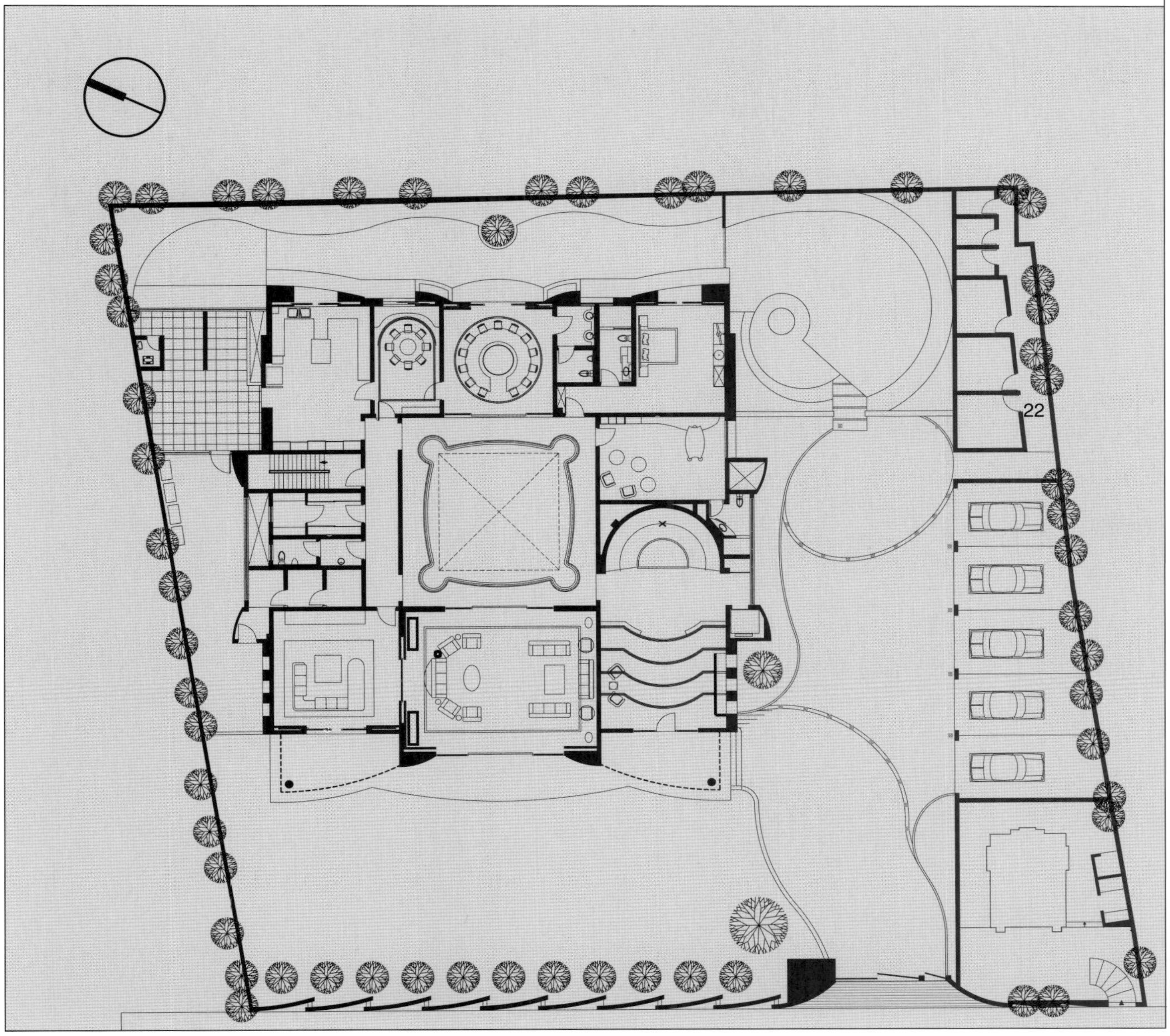

The client requirements presented several challenges – some of which at the onset, seemed impossible to satisfy. They needed a high level of security and yet, they shunned the idea of visible grills. They wanted the windows to disappear into the walls when opened. They wanted marble flooring, but without visible joints. They wanted the entire house air-conditioned, but they wanted the regular maintenance work to be carried out from outside the house. Unique demands require equally unique solutions and that is exactly what was delivered to the client resulting in a positive manifestation of the architect's creativity and expertise. The end result did not just meet the client expectations, it exceeded it.

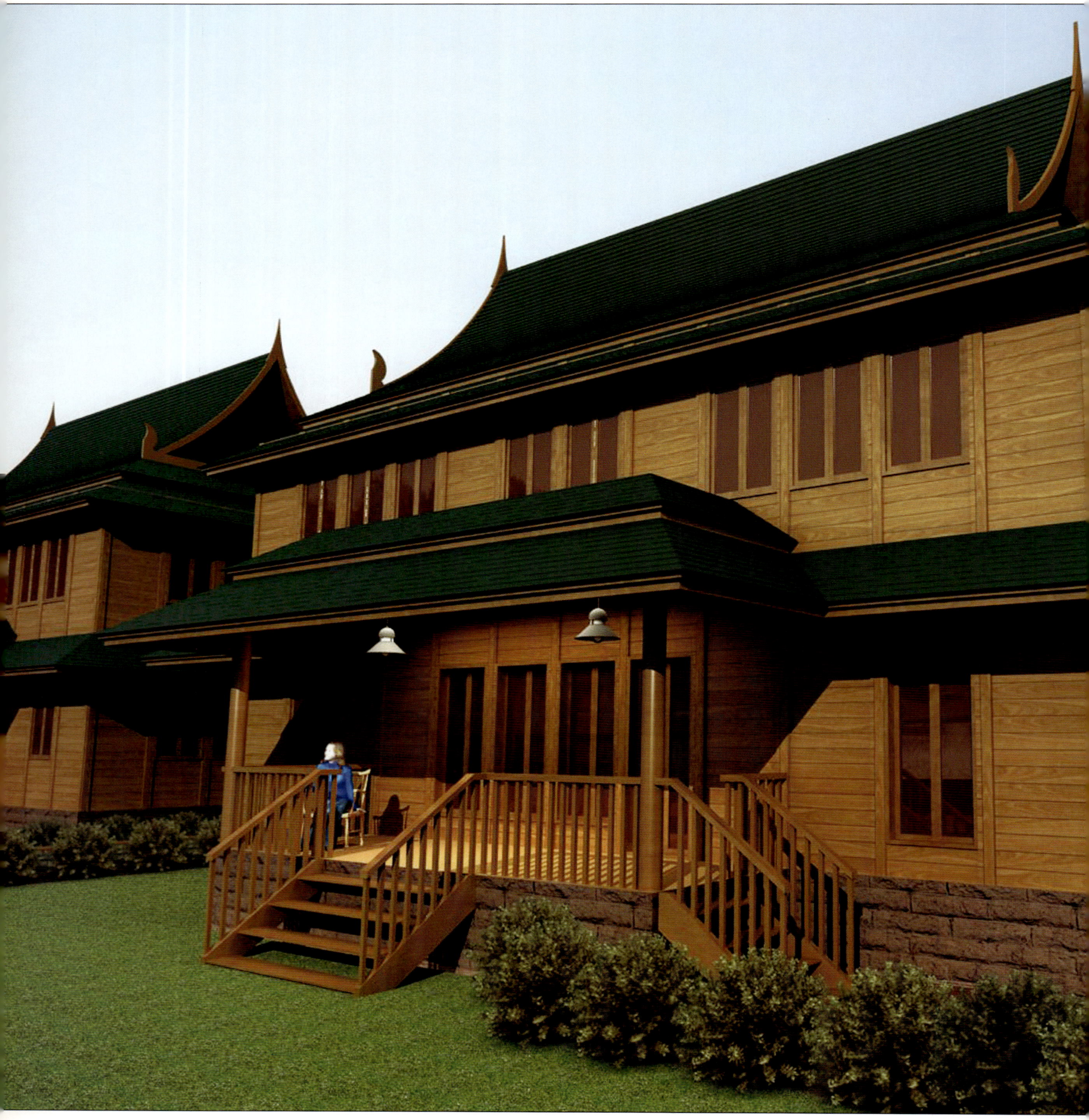

CLIENT
Timber Valley

CATEGORY
Luxury Holiday Homes

LOCATION
Lonavala, Maharashtra

PRINCIPAL ARCHITECT
Nimish Choksi

DESIGN TEAM
Vikram Bhatt
Farooq Shaikh

STRUCTURAL, MECHANICAL & ELECTRICAL
Crony Electricals

CONTRACTORS
Vikas Construction

HVAC
Jay Air Systems

FABRICATION
Patel Fabricators

PROJECT DATE
2008 – 2010

6.02 TIMBER VALLEY

This was a project proposed by Dream Properties to create exotic holiday homes in Lonavala. The architects faced two challenges. The first challenge was to make these holiday homes different from homes for living. The second challenge was the weather in Lonavala. Six months a year, work comes to a virtual standstill due to heavy rainfall. The calculations showed that it would take about four years to construct the proposed 75 villas and develop the nine-acre plot. The time factor coupled with the beautiful location, called for innovative solutions. The deadline for the project was set at 18 months. To achieve this, the houses had to be constructed somewhere else and then placed on the site, after the infrastructure was complete. The final design conceived of a foundation and plinth of the houses in reinforced concrete, the structural skeleton in steel and the skin of the house in wood. All walls of these prefabricated villas were made of Valsadi teak wood, polished and coated with special chemicals to make them water and weather resistant for years. The entire floor of the house is made out of teak wood planks, which were manufactured to specification and then easily assembled on site. Every single steel pipe required to construct the house was standardized and specified for mass-production, to be erected with nuts and bolts on the site. No welding was required for joining these steel pipes. The whole house was erected like a giant jigsaw puzzle just by bolting the prefabricated steel sections.

6.02 TIMBER VALLEY

While the idea of building wooden houses came naturally, the implementation strategy did not. The requirement for the houses to be earthquake and hurricane resistant and demands for concealed electrification, plumbing, air-conditioning, piping, etc within the wooden walls coupled with fire prevention strategies were just some of the things the architects had to give serious thought to. To counter the heavy rainfall, the skin of the house was designed as two layers. The outer wooden wall and an inner wooden wall are independent of each other. The outer wall would brave the extreme rainfall and not transfer any dampness to the inner wall. This system also concealed the steel skeleton completely and provided space for running electrical, plumbing and air-conditioning conduits. This space was then filled with an acoustic and thermal insulation material to make the house noise and heat resistant. The roof was covered with weatherproof shingles to impart a complete watertight solution.

SITE PLAN

Spacious concrete paved roads and lush green landscaping throughout the site complete the cosy picture and making this site a dream destination! The final result was a complex with a cluster of ten large villas, sixty five smaller villas, a clubhouse, a swimming pool, kids play zone, volleyball courts and a tranquil garden with a temple. All villas are also equipped with smoke detectors, fire alarms, a central fire hydrant system with fire safety equipment. A VRF air-conditioning system, which would provide cooling during summers and heating during winters has also being provided.

FIRM NAME
Niteen Parulekar Architects Pvt Ltd

ADDRESS
35 A, Madhu Industrial Estate
P B Marg, Worli
Mumbai 400013
Maharashtra

CONTACT
Tel: +91 22 66660709
www.npapl.com

My best friends are brushes, paints and canvas]

07 NITEEN PARULEKAR

A denizen of Mumbai, Niteen loved to paint as a child. Although he had the option of pursuing a career in the medical and engineering fields, his love for architecture made him join the J J College of Architecture, Mumbai. Whilst at college, Niteen discovered that he had a natural flair for perspectives and was in great demand for drawing perspectives and models by professional architects in the city. Niteen Parulekar is an architect who consistently pushes the boundaries of architecture and urban design. His work experiments with spatial quality, extending and intensifying existing landscapes in the pursuit of a visionary aesthetic that encompasses all fields of design, ranging from urban scale to products, interiors and furniture. In less than a decade, Niteen Parulekar Architects Pvt Ltd (NPAPL), with their versatile design principal has grown to a company of over 150 architects with offices in Mumbai, Pune and Delhi.

CLIENT
Panchashil Realty

CATEGORY
IT Commercial

LOCATION
Pune, Maharashtra

PRINCIPAL ARCHITECT
Niteen Parulekar

DESIGN TEAM
Iyer Venkat
Abhijeet S Nevrekar
Sumeet Kulkarni
Mangesh Brahmankar

STRUCTURAL, MECHANICAL & ELECTRICAL
S P A Consultants

MECHANICAL & ELECTRICAL
Abhiyanta Electricals

HVAC
RSK

LANDSCAPE ARCHITECTS
Ravi Gavandi & Associates

PROJECT DATE
2005 – 2008

7.01 EON

Panchshil Realty is the company behind some of the most aesthetic constructions in Pune, the IT hub of Maharashtra. When Panchshil needed a state-of-the-art design of international standards for a multi-functional, multi-tenant building targeted at the IT sector, they knew NPAPL were the architects for the job. NPAPL's design principal Niteen Parulekar and John Marx, jointly designed a horseshoe structure encompassing 4 wings, 2 in each arm of the horseshoe connecting them together, all covered under single roof, giving it an unmatched scale and presence. The structure has been placed radially from the centre of the landscaped area. The structure was envisaged in a modular fashion, such that what was applicable to one-wing would be applicable to the others as well.

7.01 EON

The roof is the most fascinating element of the design. Curving majestically, it has a sloping overhang from the exterior façade to guard the floor plate against the harsh sunlight. A rail has been added along the periphery of the overhang, enabling a cradle to be mounted on it for cleaning purposes. The security block is located at the entry, providing ample space at the head to ensure that cars awaiting security checks do not cause traffic congestion on the adjacent road. The structure hosts a two-level basement parking facility. A garden was planned at the centre of the campus to make the ambience warm and inviting. The entire complex was conceptualized using multiples of similarly structured units akin to petals coming together to create the beautiful form of a flower. An aerial view of this project looks grandiose.

SITE PLAN

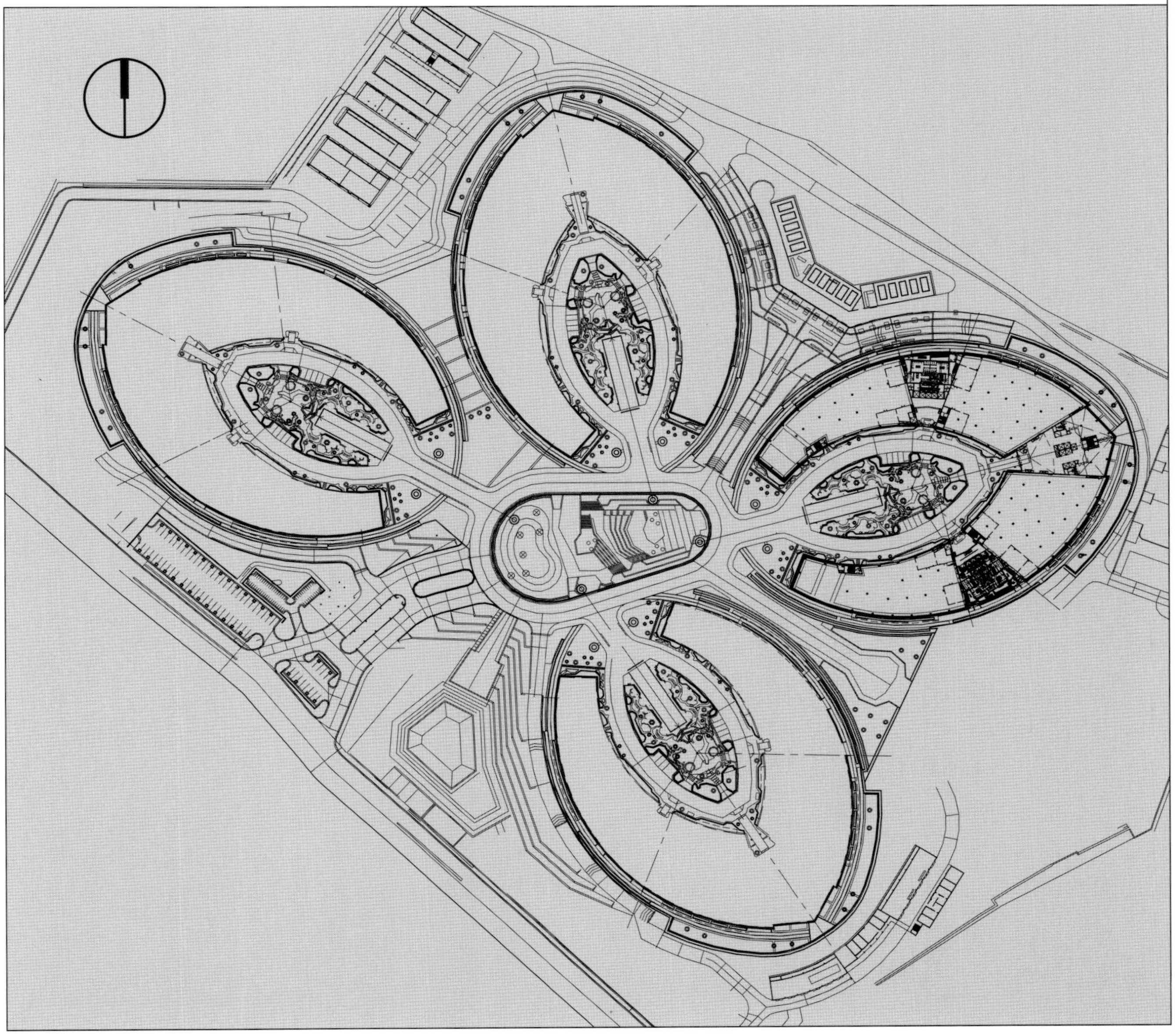

Panchshil's objective was to market the building as a flexible service oriented structure, geared towards serving a multitude of needs. NPAPL proposed a design with a curvilinear roof, a challenging task to execute. They worked with structural consultants like SPA to design the basic building frame that would support the curvilinear roof and maximize interior space. A 3D framing profile was generated in CAD and was handed over to SPA for logistical processing. A final design was jointly created and given to the contractor with uniquely numbered frames, which were post development, evaluated by SPA to ensure adherence to standards.

CLIENT
Syntel International

CATEGORY
IT Commercial

LOCATION
Pune, Maharashtra

PRINCIPAL ARCHITECT
Niteen Parulakar

DESIGN TEAM
Iyer Venkat
Abhijeet S Nevrekar
Suhas Nalawade
A John

CONTRACTORS
JMC

STRUCTURAL, MECHANICAL & ELECTRICAL
Sterling Structural Consultants
Sampat Kumar & Associates
Power Design

HVAC
Dixit Consultants

LANDSCAPE ARCHITECTS
Kishore Pradhan

PROJECT DATE
2001 – 2008

7.02 SYNTEL

Syntel's first integrated development centre was proposed in Pune, the IT hub of Maharashtra, on 40 acres of land near Indrayani. The brief was to design a centre that would reflect their goals, ideas and credibility to prospective clients in the country. The proposed plan included two software blocks, a corporate block, a food court, a dormitory and a power block among other amenities. With a location that ran along a scenic river, the plot's contours presented a unique challenge coupled with the fact that this was NPAPL's first campus development project, in a location already crammed with IT campuses.

7.02 SYNTEL

NPAPL aligned the structures based on their form and relevance. Blocks like the food court and the amphitheatre were placed next to the river to take advantage of the scenic view surrounding the site. The security block is located at the road entrance. The corporate block is placed between two software blocks along the east-west axis of the site with the elevation providing shade from the harsh sunlight. A parking lot is positioned right behind the software blocks followed by the dormitory.

SITE PLAN

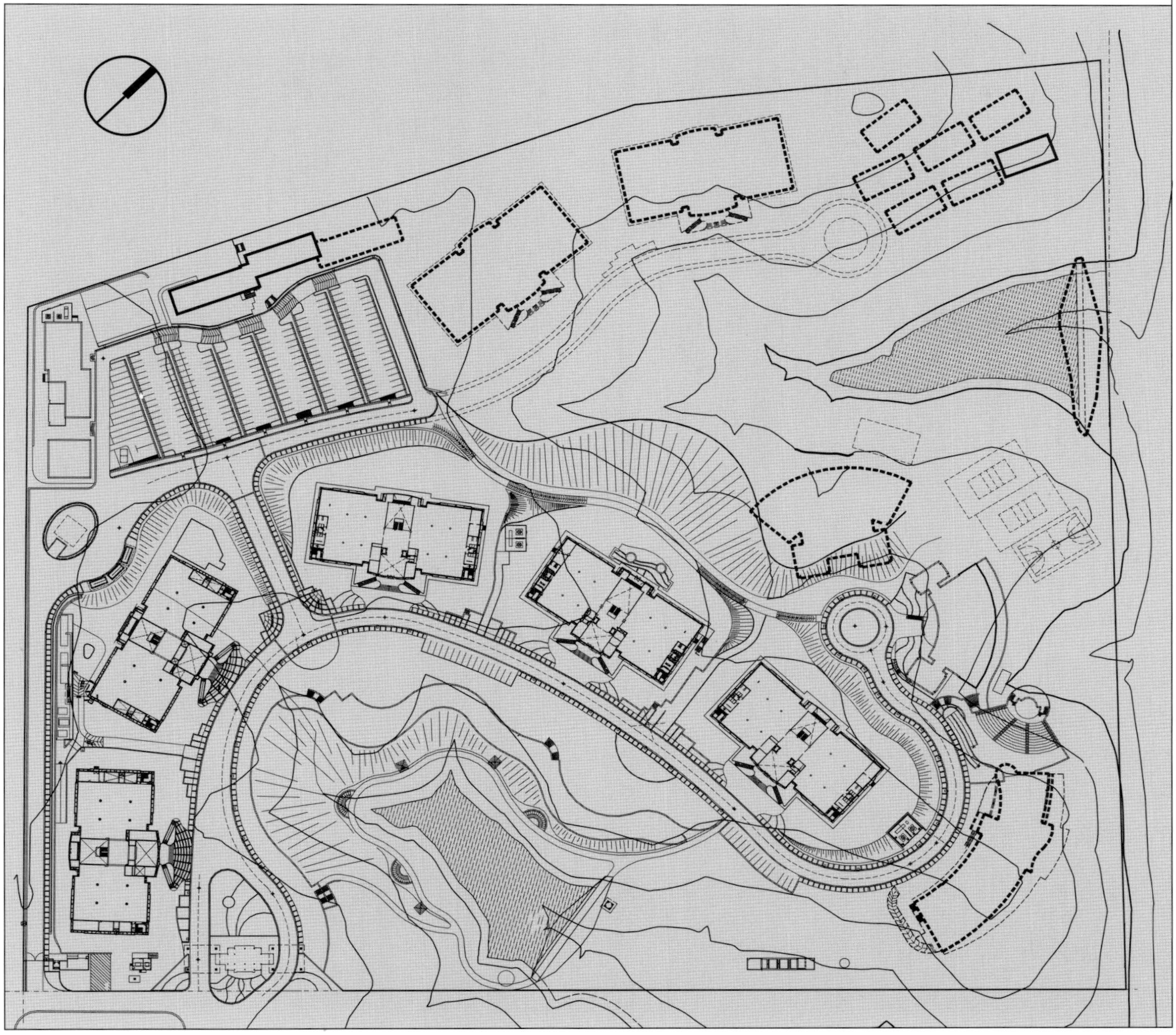

Within the campus, the reservoir is the centre of attraction. Utilizing the contours, NPAPL built a water retaining wall inside the valley towards the south side using rubble masonry. The design is institutional in its look, presented with a modern flavour to achieve the golden mean between modern and classical architecture. Creating a water retaining wall turned out to be an arduous task. A geological analysis of the site revealed a crack in the valley that was draining water far below the retaining wall. The only solution was to patch this crack using black cotton soil. Consequently a layer of it was applied across the surface of the valley to form an impervious base.

FIRM NAME
Group 7 Architects & Planners Pvt Ltd

ADDRESS
Duplex 04, N S Road
Juhu Scheme
Mumbai 400049
Maharashtra

CONTACT
Tel: +91 22 26207601
www.g7architects.com

A functional design does not have to be expensive. An intelligently designed space can lend an exciting character to any part of a city]

08 NITIN KILLAWALA

From the age of nine, Nitin Killawala was beckoned by the mysteries of blueprints, compasses, drawings and rulers that he found in his uncle's office. Nitin turned this enchantment into his career path when he joined the Bandra School of Arts (now L S Raheja College of Architecture) in Mumbai. Until recently, Nitin Killawala was the president of the Institute of Indian Interior Designers (IIID), where he worked with local authorities to provide design solutions to various infrastructure projects. Together with IIID, Nitin is working relentlessly to make a difference to our public spaces and improve its functional quality by advising and providing constructive suggestions for various infrastructure projects to bureaucrats and engineers. To Nitin, being an architect is both an inspiring and a humbling experience. "A simple line drawn and realized in space is somebody's home or livelihood. A place that they can touch, feel and cohabit in peaceful existence."

Nicholas Piramal Research Centre

CLIENT
Nicholas Piramal (I) Ltd

CATEGORY
Pharma R & D Centre

LOCATION
Goregaon, Mumbai

PRINCIPAL ARCHITECT
Nitin Killawala

DESIGN TEAM
Ketan Mistry
Samuel George

STRUCTURAL, MECHANICAL & ELECTRICAL
Sritec Consultants
Pipecon Consultants

LANDSCAPE ARCHITECTS
AMS Consultants

CONTRACTORS
Prime Contractors

PROJECT DATE
January 2004 – November 2004

8.01 NICHOLAS PIRAMAL RESEARCH CENTRE

This research centre was planned to be an aesthetically pleasing and effective workspace, a business house balancing utility with imagination. The site had an old unused structure measuring 1,20,000 sft at plinth level and 80,000 sft above, which had to be converted into a smart workspace. This Goregaon facility accommodates the process development, formulation and analytical and pharmacology laboratories including the animal house, new drug discovery section, corporate offices, employee amenities as well as service areas. A tangy orange façade, reflecting the company's corporate colour, along with white was chosen to give an elegant and welcoming appearance. The main entrance in white is dominated by a series of tensile structures that hover above the facade representing the company's progressive ideas and their unrelenting zeal for perfection.

8.01 NICHOLAS PIRAMAL RESEARCH CENTRE

An amalgamation of thoughtfully designed spaces and innovative planning has ensured that the research centre and the corporate offices coexist in perfect harmony. The design layout ensures that all sections are strategically and suitably placed. The toxic fumes emitting organic chemistry lab is placed in a section of the building that has ample ventilation. Formulation and analytical laboratories requiring artificial regulation of the environment with no natural light or ventilation, are planned with a dead wall at the core of the building. Each section is also colour-coded to provide each workspace with a definite distinction. For example, the circulation area uses Jaisalmer yellow flooring while the pharmacology lab is identified by its blue interiors. The corporate offices are equipped with state-of-the-art meeting rooms, a friendly cafeteria, an auditorium and a library. With walls adorning the works of Eriko Horiki, a Japanese artist and Dr Swati Piramal, the overall effect created is both tranquil and overwhelming. Running water matched with the colour black adds to the volume of this existing space and creates a composed setting.

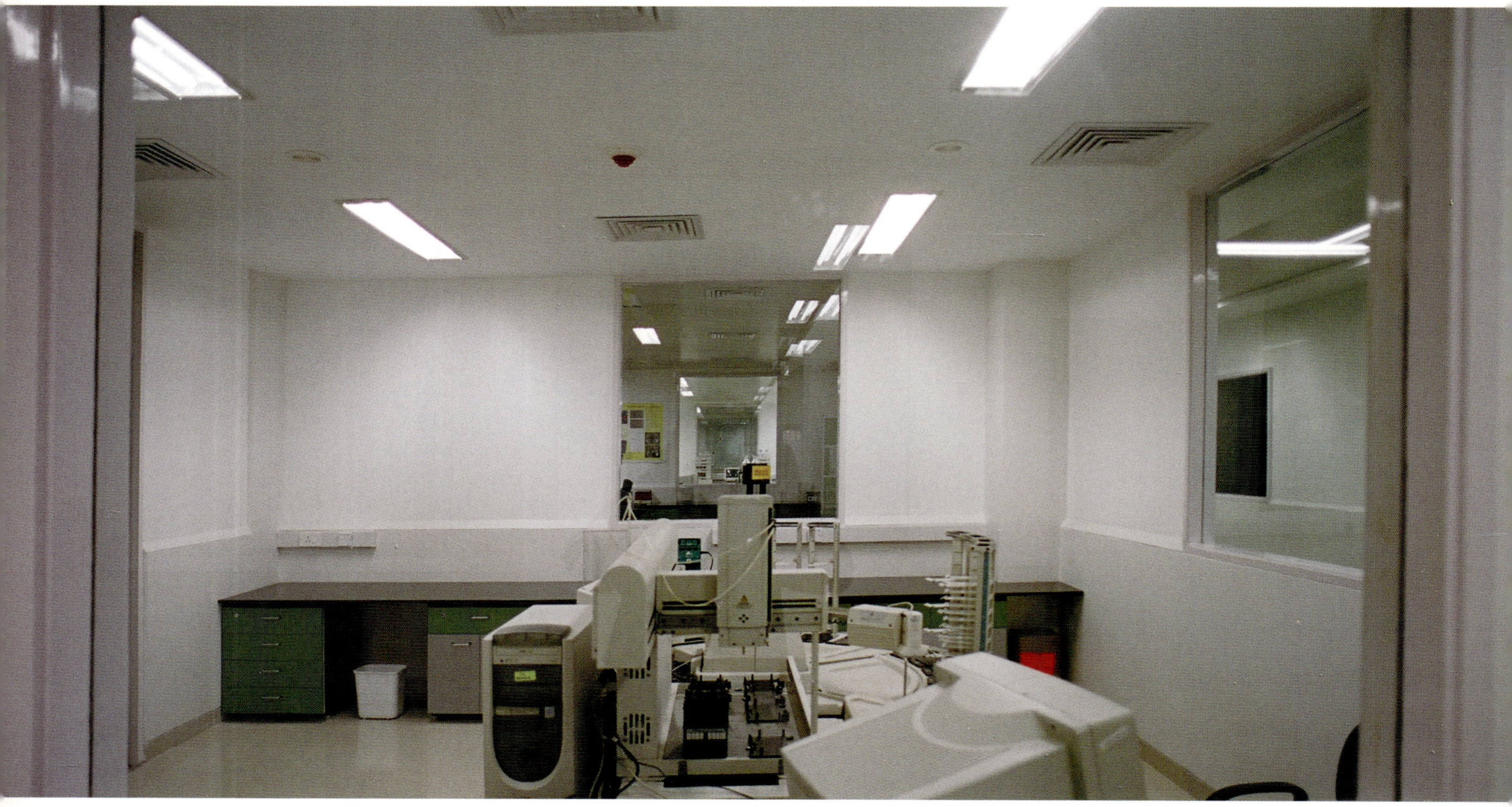

SITE PLAN

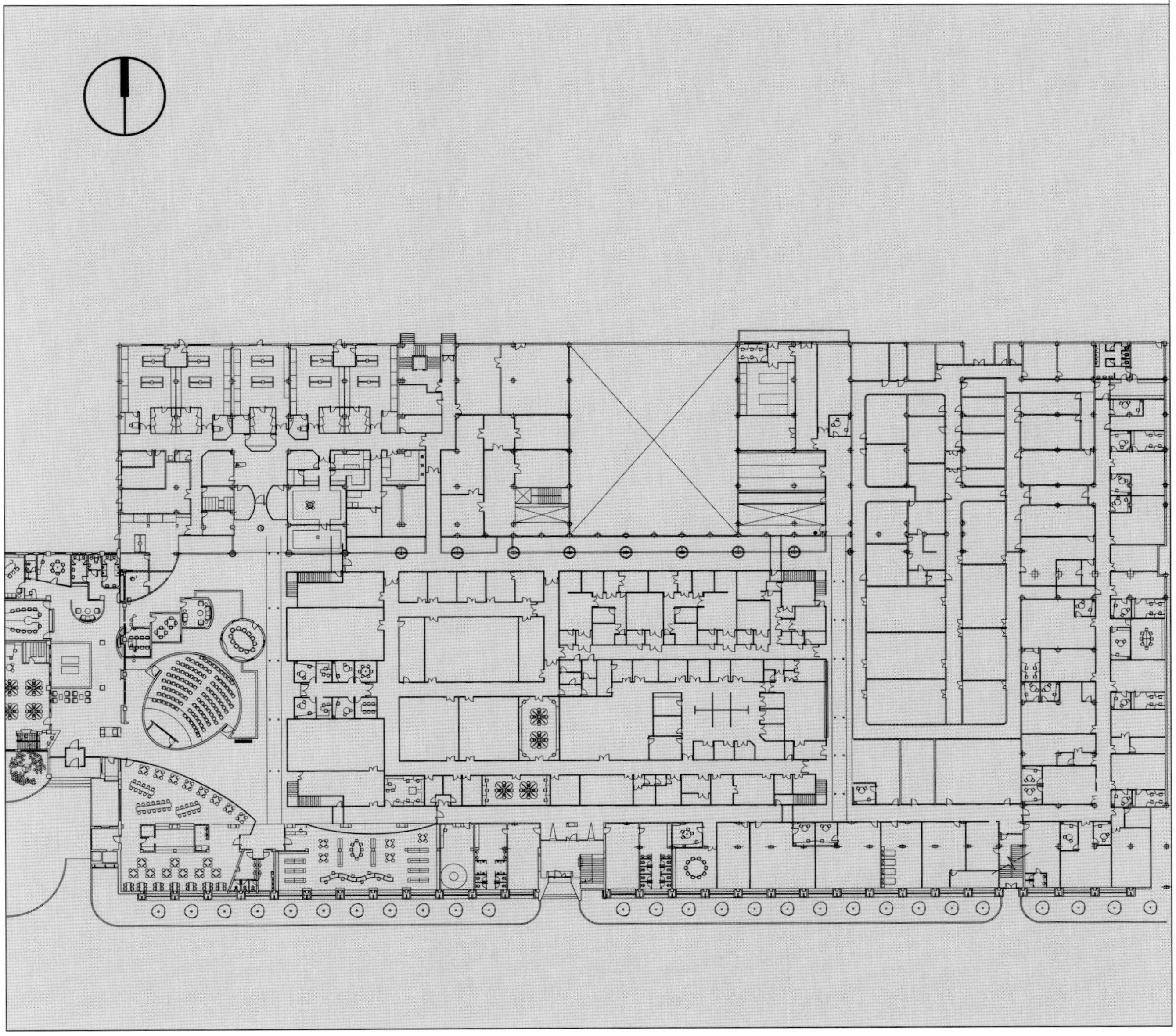

To emphasise safety, each lab section is transparent allowing employees to keep a watch on the other lab sections. Bridges have been designed to connect labs and offices providing ease of movement among the vast interiors. Patios located within the heart of the building enable natural light filtering, providing warmth to the facility. Main architectural and structural accomplishment is the 70,000 sft column of free space, which provides a double-height volume allowing filtered light to penetrate into the deep interiors of the building. It also lends a degree of transparency to the remote sections of the building, which helps employees in one section to stay connected with those in other sections and gives the structure an impression of a single large unit. The planning of this facility has also taken care of future enhancements to the building in an intelligent and creative manner.

CLIENT
Killawala family

CATEGORY
Resort House

LOCATION
Foothills of Matheran, Maharashtra

PRINCIPAL ARCHITECT
Nitin KIllawala

CONTRACTORS
Ismail & Co

STRUCTURAL, MECHANICAL & ELECTRICAL
Sritec Consultants
Richard Electricals

LANDSCAPE ARCHITECTS
AMS Consultants

PROJECT DATE
1994 – 1995

8.02 TRIKALYAM

The architect's intention was to create a vacation home on this 1 acre of land which was situated in a small village barely 60 kms from Mumbai. They wanted a home with only the bare essentials without the trappings of modern amenities. Air-conditioners are replaced by huge windows, which dominate the space bringing in fresh air and enchanting view frames reflecting the changing seasons. The site was just a barren plot with dense forestation, abundant beautiful valleys all around and a water body adjacent to the land with loads of trees close to the property.

8.02 TRIKALYAM

The house is planned without a designated front or back as all four sides of this structure have scenic openings. The ceiling stands tall at 22 ft, making the living room appear more spacious and ventilated. The steel and iron louvers cross-ventilate the house adequately. The house is built using load bearing stones carved from the mountains close to this region. Traditional materials like bamboo sticks are also imaginatively used to take maximum advantage of filtered ventilation. Nitin's artistic use of local materials such as unplastered slabs and the red-oxide flooring gives this home an eternal authentic touch. The living room has been designed keeping the taste of all family members in mind. Small concerts are held in this home on occasions to keep the family in touch with their ancestral roots. Original handicrafts have been tastefully used to enhance the beauty and simplicity of the basic design. To increase the intimacy in scale, the window and the floor level have been created at lower than the normal standards.

FLOOR PLAN

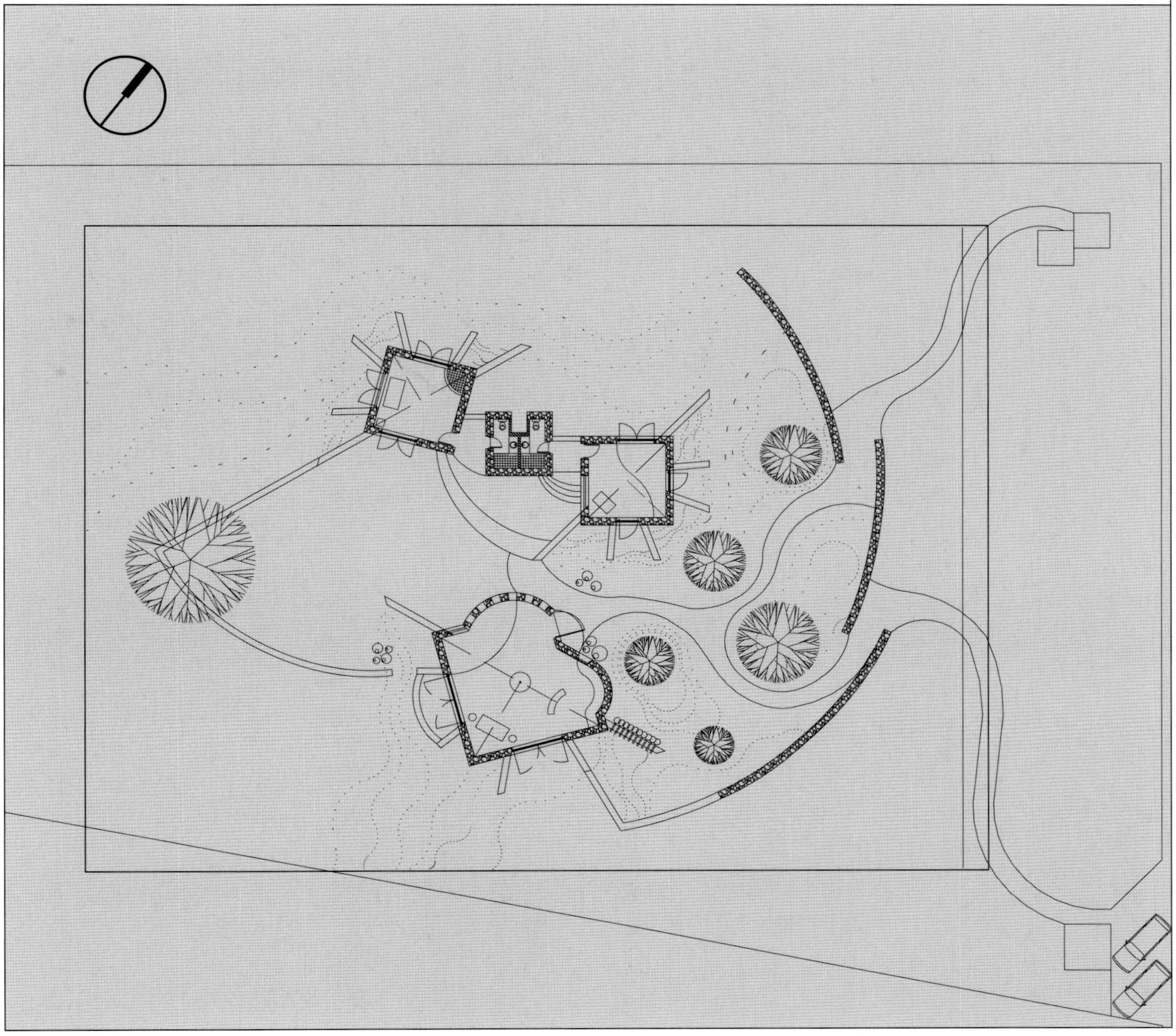

This environment-friendly home has a 115 ft high white tower housing a wind mill that generates electricity for the house by harnessing wind power. The toilet is built underneath. Sleeping rooms have been designed to provide maximum privacy. However, no curtains prevent nature from peeping into the large windows. The bedroom also has a sunken shower. A deck has been created as an extension of the living space with a 60 ft long bridge leading up to it, creating a place fit for discussions and nostalgic indulgences. The water tank and the toilet block are placed right in the middle of the house, thus saving additional space required for the tank tower, while achieving strong and clear water pressure in the showers at 35 ft N. "When you see sunlight with the backdrop of mountains, green trees and abundant water, it creates a sense of drama and transports you into a mindset very different from our everyday lives. This mind set is inspiring and helps our family and friends reinvent themselves and their ideas consistently."

FIRM NAME
Prem Nath & Associates

ADDRESS
S-288A, Panchashila Park
New Delhi 110017

CONTACT
Tel: +91 11 26014251
www.premnath.com

Architecture infuses life into buildings. It satisfies the creative soul. It encourages us to keep abreast of lifestyle, trends and technology. It forces us to think ahead, for we are responsible for guiding our clients]

09 PREM NATH

Prem Nath studied architecture from the J J School of Architecture, Mumbai. Graduating with a Gold Medal and equipped with his natural talent for mathematics, science, and graphic arts, he learnt the practical aspects of architecture as an intern with Karim Noorani & Associates. He believes that clients know what they want and he, as an expert in spaces, knows exactly what they need. He describes his architectural approach as functional as he believes that a structure should serve the purpose for which it is being built. All else is secondary. His creations are iconic structures of the Mumbai skyline. These include Hotel Ambassador, Hotel Sea Rock, Nehru Planetarium and Hare Krishna Temple to name a few. While designing & planning his buildings, he does not believe in '*Vastu Shastra*'. According to him it does not exist in the form of *shastras* (ancient scriptures). "That scripture", he says, "is a figment of somebody's imagination." Highly respected by his colleagues and clients for his functional and unique designs, Prem Nath is an enthusiastic member of the American Society of Interior Designers and a fellow of the Institution of Engineers (India) Chartered Engineers. He has also served as the President of the Indian Institute of Interior Designers and finds mention in the international edition of Who's Who in Interior Design. He has also won the Architect of the Year Award in 1996 from Accommodation Times, the International Award of Architectural Practice in 2005 from Actualidad, Spain.

CLIENT
World Resorts Ltd

CATEGORY
Luxury Resort & Health spa

LOCATION
Bengaluru, Karnataka

PRINCIPAL ARCHITECT
Prem Nath

DESIGN TEAM
Studio Group II

CONTRACTORS
Arshad Construction

STRUCTURAL, MECHANICAL & ELECTRICAL
Chetna Consortium

LANDSCAPE ARCHITECTS
A Mohan, Jimmy Amrolia

PROJECT DATE
1997 – 2001

9.01 GOLDEN PALMS

This 5-star luxurious health resort and spa has been designed keeping international standards in mind. Prem Nath has been involved in this project right from the consulting phase to the final development stage. It is designed to provide relaxation and health conscious programmes for the highly stressed, highly placed individuals, corporate executives and the elite who seek body and mind relaxation in serene and exotic settings. Prem Nath, keeping in mind the profile of the visitors, kept comfort as his core concept. Good food, good ambience, expert guidance and the opportunity to lose weight and rejuvenate were some of the facilities that were planned for the guests. With these requirements, he decided to develop this 14-acre farmland property and gave it a face of a luxury resort. The resort plan was to host 150 deluxe rooms and suites along with restaurants, bars, cafés, banquets, conference rooms, sports facilities and a business centre.

9.01 GOLDEN PALMS

The design covers facilities and programmes from basic diagnostic check up, stress reduction, physical treatments, including beauty and cosmetic centres and body enhancement facilities, a central large pool and landscaped gardens with fountains and sculptures. Guest rooms, cottages, grand reception hall and spa, are all planned and placed strategically. The pool is the central feature of the resort. About 492 ft long, in a serpentine free form lagoon, it is touted as one of the largest pools in Asia, with a separate section for play pool, deck, water sports, a pool bridge with water jets for aqua aerobics and just plain cool water for the laid-back guests. The poolside café with a large poolside deck with a separate poolside bar and barbecue grill offers opportunity for sunbathing and also for recreational activities with floor shows and other entertainment. The interiors have been skillfully accomplished by Zarine Khan with floral design fabrics, cane, bamboo, iron and rustic wood with health based artworks and artifacts. Prem Nath, in coordination with Jimmy Amrolia and A Mohan, has completed the fabulous landscapes, plant-scapes and horticulture complete with its maintenance.

SITE PLAN

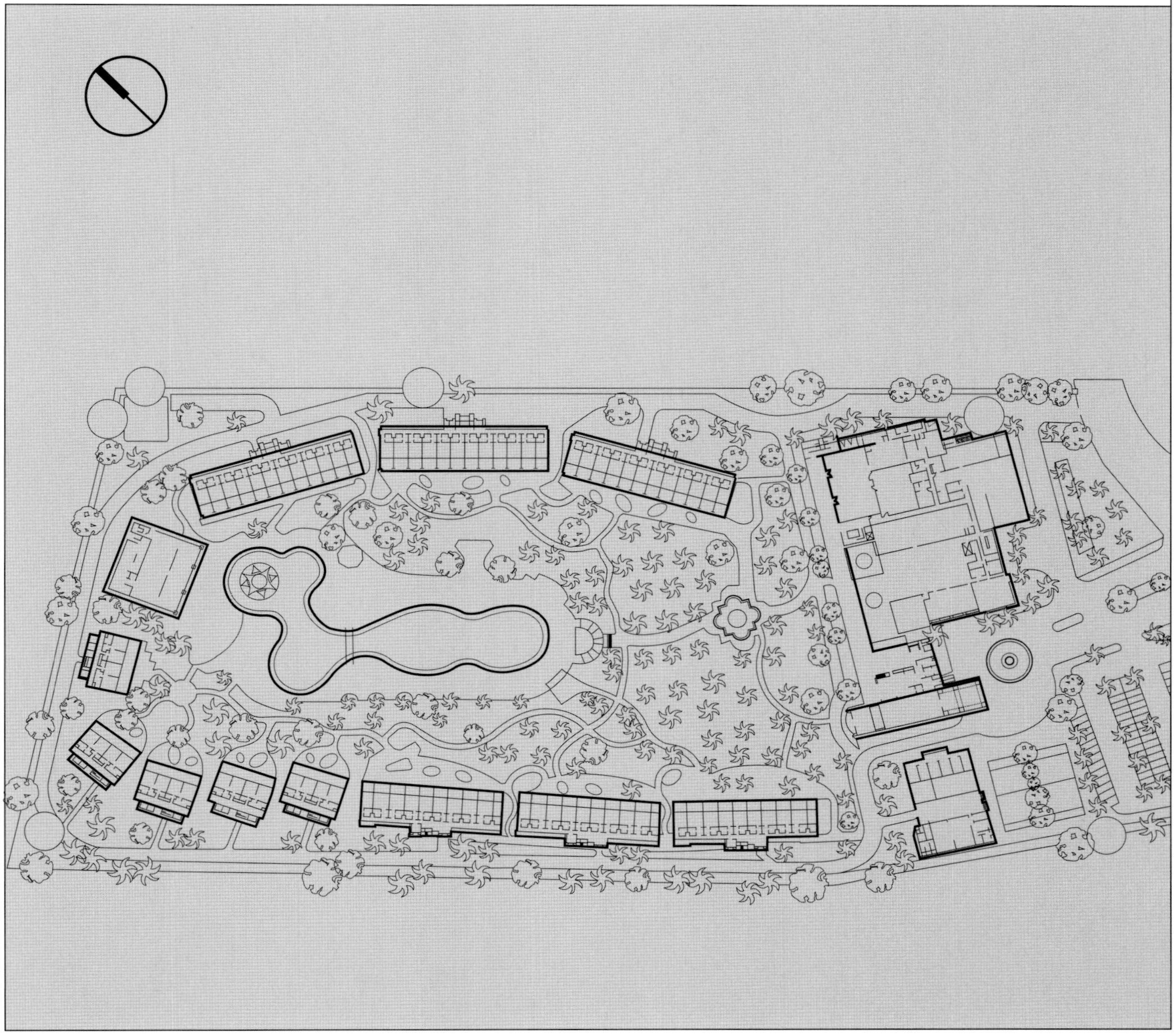

All guest rooms and cottages have attached verandahs overlooking the gardens and patios. The rooms have been designed as ground-plus-one storey 20-room modules, while the cottages are ground-plus-one storey 8-room modules. A separate sports building and sports zone house all the major indoor and outdoor games along with a sports bar lounge, sports shop, health food outlets and a boutique. No vehicles are allowed within the complex, except in the parking zone. Since the development is planned horizontally, all internal movements are accomplished by go-carts for transporting visitors or baggages. Trees and features have been illuminated with floor embedded and trunk mounted concealed lights. The architecture is heavily influenced by the Mediterranean – rustic abode look with stucco plaster for all interior and exterior walls. Flooring, is terracotta ceramic tiles, slate and local rough hand dressed granite and cobblestone for pavement and driveways. Roofing façade has been treated with local country pan tiles. The colours are terracotta, sepia, earthy peach and off white. The spa, therefore, has an earthy tranquil atmosphere which encourages the visitors to connect with nature and themselves.

Citi Mall
ADLABS

CLIENT
Ajmera Group

CATEGORY
Multiplex and Shopping Mall

LOCATION
Mumbai, Maharashtra

PRINCIPAL ARCHITECT
Prem Nath

DESIGN TEAM
General Studio Group II

CONTRACTORS
Ajmera Builders

STRUCTURAL, MECHANICAL & ELECTRICAL
Satish Dhupelia, Ketan Shah

LANDSCAPE ARCHITECTS
Prem Nath & Associates

PROJECT DATE
2001 – 2002

9.02 CITI MALL

A five-screen multiplex and a shopping mall, Citi Mall Multiplex is situated in Andheri, Mumbai. A first-of-its kind in Mumbai, Prem Nath designed this 1,61,458 sft area in approximately 18 months. Using 64,583 sft of space, the building design has been worked as 217 ft x 138 ft building block with five theatres of 43 ft x 98 ft with a seating capacity of 330. The lounge and restrooms cover approximately 197 ft x 40 ft of space. Counters for snacks and drinks are placed in suitable places. The layout is an excellent example of an architect's skill to provide a simple, efficient and cost effective solution, which also provides space that most cine goers look forward to. In addition, the multiplex has one common linear projector room, which enables a single operator to run and manage all five different movies with different projectors. All theatres have been incorporated with a soft sound fabric fused with absorption panels on side walls, with dimmer controlled lighting to enhance the sound effects.

9.02 CITI MALL

A centrally air-conditioned shopping centre comprises of over 400 shopping modules of approximately 161 sft each. The shopping area has separate service stairs and service freight lifts, fire exits etc. There is provision for about 400 car parking spaces in the complex. The exterior of the mall is finished in jade green aluminium cladded panels & structural glazing. The lower floor is finished in steel grey granite cladding. All interior finishing is done with vitrified floor tiles for shops and Italian marble for common public area and interior wall claddings. The overall effect is one of grandeur and a space which invites the cine goers to have a comfortable and enjoyable experience.

FLOOR PLAN

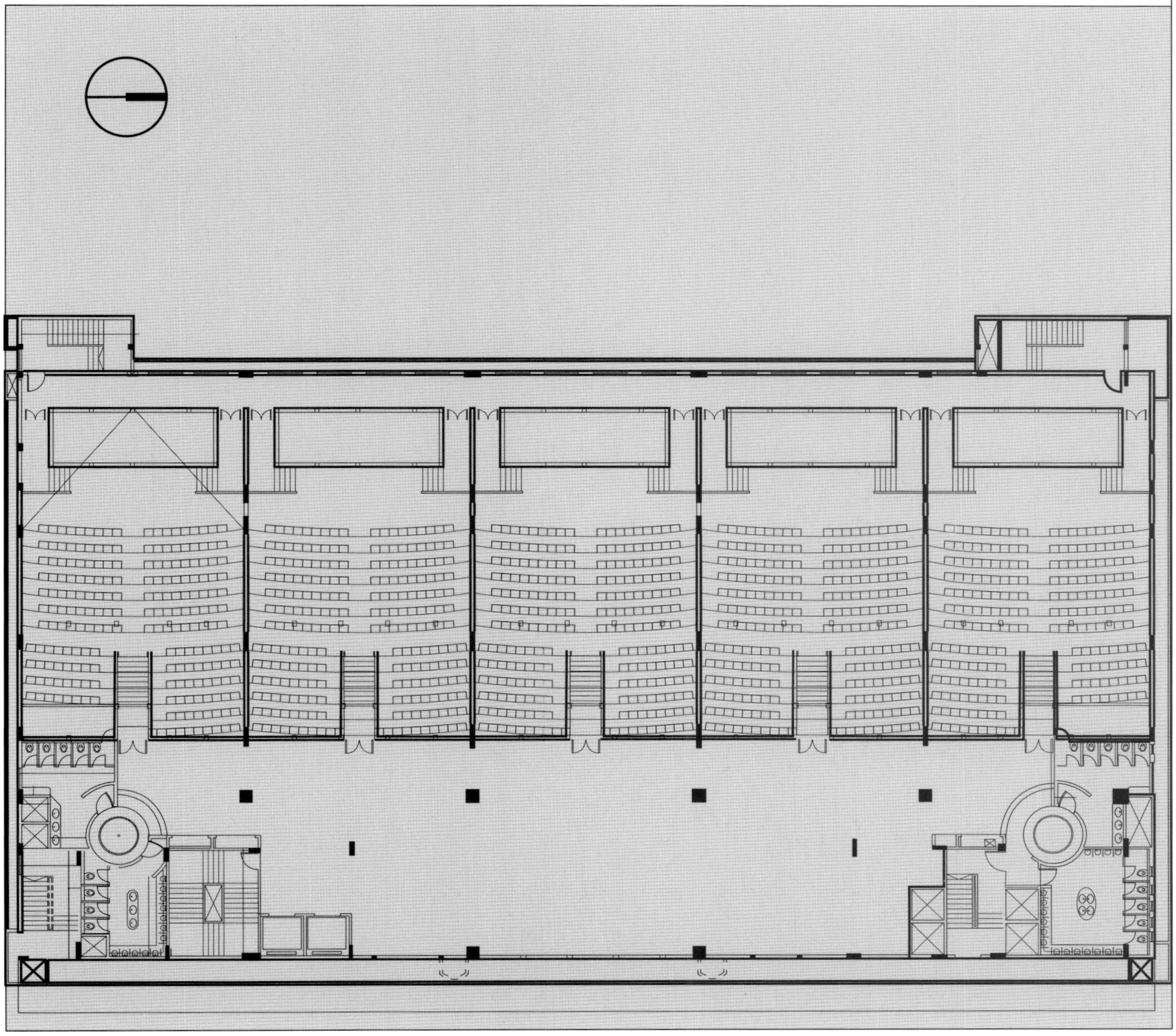

Since this was the first of its kind multiplex in the country, the main challenge was not the structure or the design but it was that of educating the personnel at the execution & operational level. Even the approving authorities had to be guided on various norms and principles of planning. Furthermore circulation, multiple ticketing, e-ticketing and complex timelines of screening were conceived in the most functional manner – providing a large lounge hall common to all screens and with appropriate software / IT technology. Citi Mall project also incorporates shopping & offices. It was also important to create a sound barrier between screening halls & these spaces. While developing any such first, the architect needs to be one-up, has to self-educate, then further improve and lay the foundations for planning so as to establish certain norms for others to follow.

FIRM NAME
Rajinder Kumar Associates

ADDRESS
B-6/17, Shopping Centre
Safdarjung Enclave
New Delhi 110029

CONTACT
Tel: +91 11 26162930 / 31
www.rka.in

Design over the years has changed in form and function. It has been absorbed by everyday culture, and we have to keep those constants in mind]

10 RAJINDER KUMAR

Rajinder Kumar completed his studies in architecture from the Delhi Polytechnic Institute. After graduation, he joined architect Le Corbusier's team in Chandigarh. Having worked with a world renowned architect during his formative years was a unique and deeply enriching experience. In 1965, he joined Choudhary & Gulzarsingh in Delhi, where Rajinder got an opportunity to hone his skills further. He headed the design team for the Ashoka Hotels in Delhi. He was also an integral part of the beautification of the city for which he designed the Inter State Bus Terminal, his first project in collaboration with the New Delhi Municipal Corporation. In 1970, he started his own firm, Rajinder Kumar Associates (RKA). A landmark opportunity for RKA was the invitation to design the US Naval Base in Philippines. The World Bank, impressed with his body of work, offered him this project. Rajinder headed a team of worldwide consultants of transportation & ecology among others. He redesigned 15,000 hectares of land and converted it into a civilian facility. The then mayor of Philippines, Mr Richard Gordon praised Rajinder Kumar highly for his efforts and excellent work.

MART
Mart
Halls
CFB
Mart Side Entrances

CLIENT
India Exposition Mart Ltd

CATEGORY
Exhibition Centre

LOCATION
Vasant Kunj, New Delhi

PRINCIPAL ARCHITECT
Rajinder Kumar

DESIGN TEAM
Rahul Kumar
Narender Gupta

STRUCTURAL, MECHANICAL & ELECTRICAL
Semac

UTILITIES
Sunil Khanna (Kitchen Consultants)
LSI India (Facade Lighting)

CONTRACTORS
Ahluwalia Contracts

HVAC
Consultant – Spectral

LANDSCAPE ARCHITECTS
Design Cell

PROJECT DATE
2002 – 2006

10.01 INDIA EXPO MART LIMITED

India Expo Mart Ltd (IEML) wanted a platform in India of international standards to hold exhibitions, conventions and seminars, thus serve to explore business opportunities, technology transfer, investment and other areas of business co-operation with buyers from all over the world. In addition, the site would host fairs and exhibitions to facilitate interaction between buyers and government officials from various ministries, trade associations and the Chamber of Commerce. Rajinder Kumar and his team were given a brief that this site should emulate the spirit of round-the-clock marts in Dallas and Atlanta in the USA, Utrecht in the Netherlands and Shanghai in China. The centre was to be designed to accommodate convention centres, exhibition halls, transportation facilities, hotels, business centres, restaurants, conference halls and even helipads – all in one location. This site also had to be available 24/7/365 days of the year. Potential buyers, investors and wholesalers coming from overseas were to have all their requirements fulfilled, all year long, at one destination.

10.01 INDIA EXPO MART LIMITED

The project was initiated in phases. Currently, Phase I is complete & operational. Phase II is nearing completion and the development of Phase III has commenced. The built-up area of Phase I and II is approximately 16,14,586 sft. The proposed built-up area of Phase III is approximately 9,14,932 sft. The centre has large exhibition halls, a trade mart, convention centres, hotel, offices, food courts, banks, meeting rooms, crate storage, warehouse, truck docks and banquet facilities. Built close to the highway, the innovative use of large solid walls of red and beige local sand stone, along with the use of clear glass and aluminium panels makes this building a strong landmark in Noida / Greater Noida areas of Uttar Pradesh. There is a central function building spread over approximately 1,08,715 sft which provides functional facilities such as the reception, registration area, VIP lounge, central security room, office area, meeting rooms, conference halls, banquet halls, F&B outlets, kiosks, food courts, restaurants, post office, courier services, banks, foreign exchange, shipping companies, travel & hotel agents, tourist companies and car rentals. A support / service area has been provided which includes a guest house, club, gymnasium, warehouses, office complex and space for all utility systems among others. There is also a parking facility for 2,000 cars and 200 trucks.

Level B,C,D
CFB
Mart

NO SMOKING

FLOOR PLAN

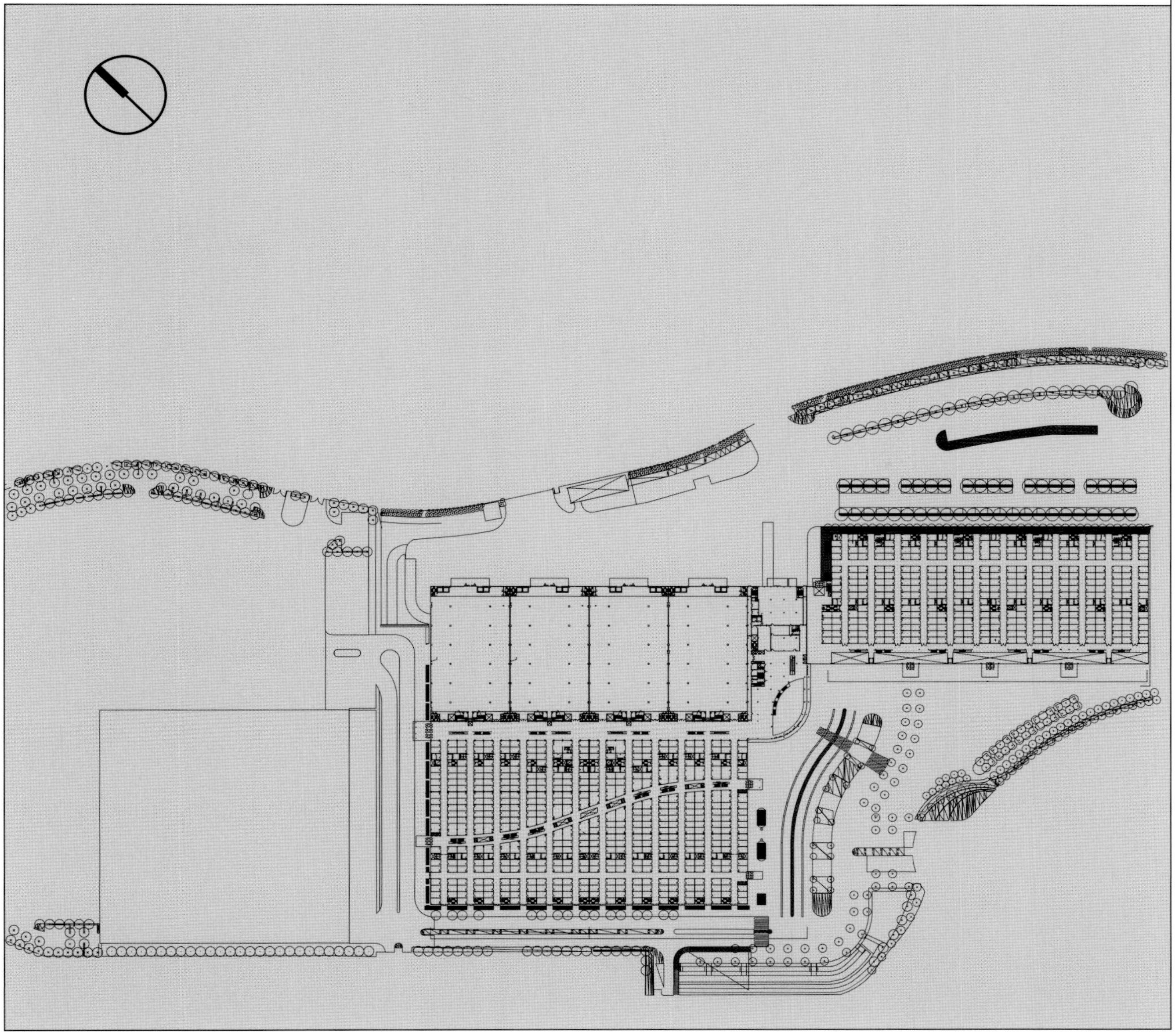

The sole aim of the team while building this project was to provide a world class facility to businessmen / women to showcase their products and generate business opportunity. The sheer scale of the structure combined with a limited time-frame and budget constraints made execution a real challenge. Multilevel halls further complicated the structure. The maximum height of the structure was pegged at 59 ft by statute for steel structures which was a significant restriction considering the structure was meant to serve as an exhibition hall. Furthermore, the site was placed on a high water table requiring the construction of a retention bond system designed to collect rain water. Based in the vicinity of the Greg Norman Golf Course, IEML has been a prominent architectural icon, playing a major role in the development of the location. Designed with the highest standards in functionality, its grand architecture commands higher visibility making it the focal point for large scale exhibitions. Its presence has transcended the Noida region to encompass the entire NCR region.

CLIENT
ITC Ltd

CATEGORY
Training Centre

LOCATION
Gurgaon, Haryana

PRINCIPAL ARCHITECT
Rajinder Kumar

DESIGN TEAM
Rahul Kumar
Ramesh Koul

STRUCTURAL, MECHANICAL & ELECTRICAL
V G Associates

CONTRACTORS
Ahluwalia Contracts

HVAC
ECE

LANDSCAPE ARCHITECTS
Design Cell

PROJECT DATE
2002 – 2005

10.02 ITC GREEN CENTRE

The ITC Green Centre at Gurgoan is yet another landmark that houses offices of ITC's varied business. A platinum rated green building certified under the LEEDS certification program, this building has become the face of the new and trendy Gurgaon. The 1,80,000 sft area has been developed keeping in mind ITC's corporate culture, their civic pride and commitment to constantly improving their surroundings. Backed by extensive research, the team of architects and engineers worked with diligence and perseverance to translate a vision into reality. The end result – a piece of architectural history. The ITC Centre is located close to the national highway connecting New Delhi and Gurgaon. A composition of three parts, the building has two office wings, held together by a central atrium. The atrium is an L-shaped block, which ensures that a part of the façade always remains shaded. These office wings merge into hexagonal ends that make an impressive structure. The atrium connects different functions of the structure. Free natural light illuminates the atrium section without allowing heat to penetrate the roof.

10.02 ITC GREEN CENTRE

A glazed office front ensures natural light and a beautiful view of the landscapes from the offices. Tall ceilings, large windows, no VOC's in paints, adhesives or sealants ensure high quality indoor air in all areas at all times. The creative combination of a solid stone base and glass projects the company's stability and dignity. The red brick with the white sandstone base gives this building an impressive visual enhancement. The landscape of this building is distinctive. A 100% water harvesting provision, 0% run off and recycling of irrigation water ensures that very little water is used to keep the beautiful landscape green. Energy efficient lighting (T5 Lamps with electronic ballast), high efficient luminaries, water efficient landscaping, carbon dioxide monitoring, indoor chemical and pollutant source control, indoor air quality system, optimised energy performance through efficient designs, light pollution reduction, ozone protection, water-use reduction and storm water management, makes this building an e-building – sensitive to the environment, making this the most energy efficient building in India.

GROUND FLOOR PLAN

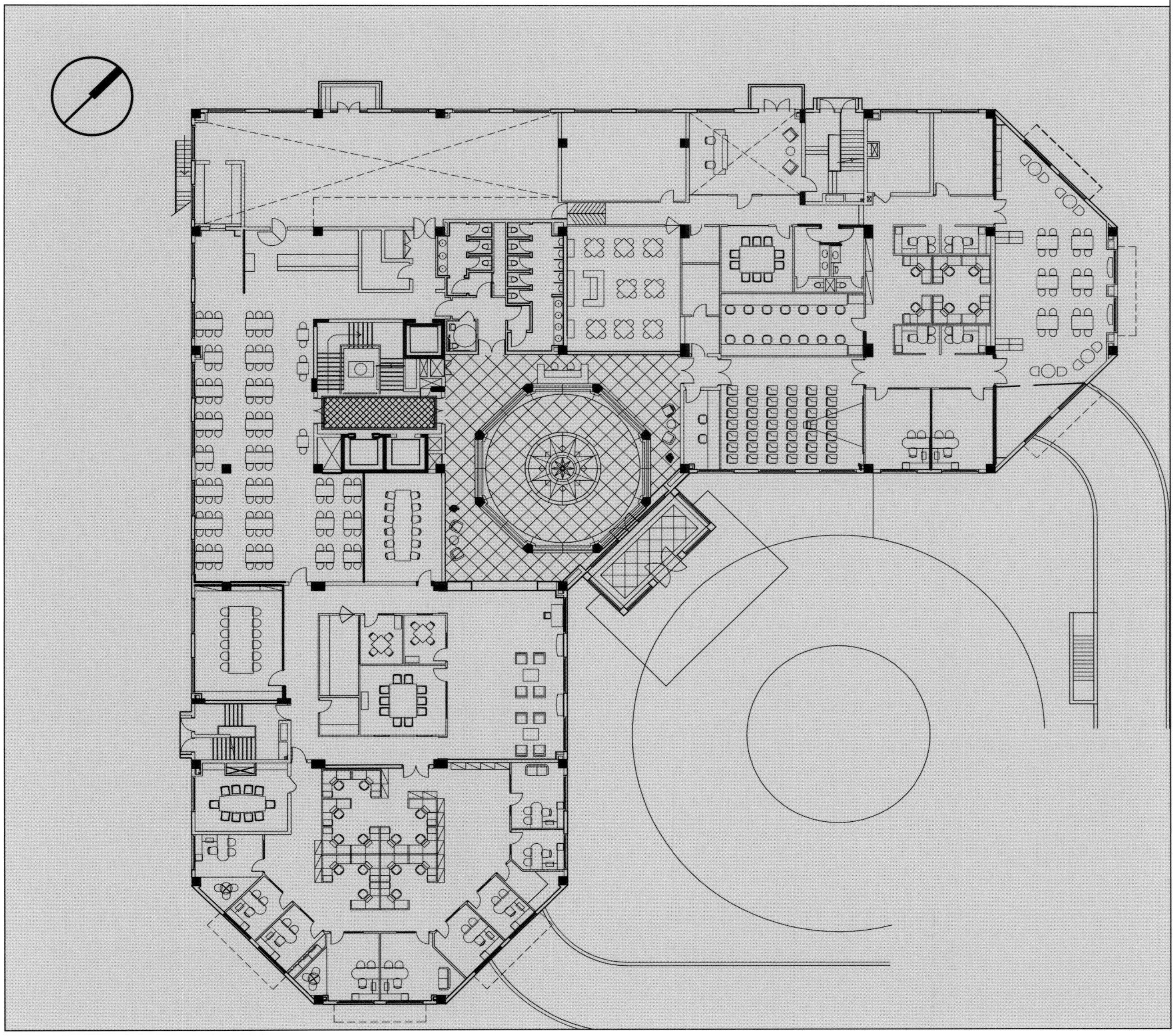

Creating a green building was not part of the original specification. The specification was modified to include the green element when the design process was well underway. Extensive research had to be conducted on existing norms in energy modeling and platinum rating standards. It was the first attempt to create a large green building which, in addition to serving its primary purpose as a corporate structure, had to be rated platinum. Without existing structures in the category, the team relied on exhaustive enquiry into the science of green architecture. Furthermore, ITC, a company with unparalleled goodwill, was uncompromising in its demand that the structure, even though a first of its kind, was not to look experimental in any aspect. The structure, they felt, should project a maturity worthy of the ITC brand. The end result not only met these demands, but exceeded them in many ways through synergy and coordination amongst the various specialists that came together to create this one-of-a-kind structure.

FIRM NAME
ARK Consultants Pvt Ltd

ADDRESS
Plot No 78-A, 2nd Floor
Turner Road, Bandra (W)
Mumbai 400050
Maharashtra

CONTACT
Tel: +91 22 26439415
www.architectrezakabul.com

High-rises enable individuals to work and spend time with family and friends within the same premises, eliminating the need to travel, saving time and raising the standard of living, besides being environmentally friendly. The modern high-rise, in essence, is a mini-city]

11 REZA KABUL

Reza Kabul studied architecture from Maharaja Sayaji Rao University, Vadodara. After graduating, he joined Architect Hafeez Contractor. There, among his ambitious and innovative colleagues, learning the ropes in just two short years, Reza quit and decided to go independent. He started by creating his workspace at his father's restaurant in Worli. He started with buildings and interiors in Thane, Kalyan and Badlapur. In 1989, he got his first big break when he was asked to design an 18-storey tower in Byculla, Mumbai. Reza Kabul turned the Roger's Rasberry Soda factory to the sophisticated Sagar Classic. He is also the man behind the design of the 206-room five star, Le Meridian, in Mauritius. Some of his major achievements include the Shreepati Arcade – India's tallest building, listed in the Limca Books of Records 2003. He has also been honoured with The Best Architect of the year award, 2004 by Accommodation Times, Gun Gaurav Puraskar (Best Performance) by Practising Engineers, Architects Town Planners Association (PEATA) in 2005. He has also been awarded by various other groups for his outstanding work viz "Host 2007" by H&FS for best hotel room designed, by The Economic Times in 2007 and by MCHI in 2005. Reza's portfolio features a range of architectural and interior projects in India, Dubai, Afghanistan, Muscat, Abu Dhabi, Ras-al-Khaimah and Mauritius. Currently Reza is working on the 85-storey high Shreepati Skies which will be one of the tallest residential buildings in India.

RAGHULEELA
Welcome to a
Unique Shopping
Experience
WEDNESDAY
BAZAAR
Ab wholesale
prices me in
ghar chaloo

CLIENT
Wadhwa Group

CATEGORY
Shopping Mall

LOCATION
Vashi, Maharastra

PRINCIPAL ARCHITECT
Reza Kabul

DESIGN TEAM
Vaishali Jian Solanki
Akbar Maredia

STRUCTURAL, MECHANICAL & ELECTRICAL
Niranjan Pandya
Geodesic Techniques
MEP Consultants

CONTRACTORS
Gajanan Associates

FACADE & GLAZING
Aluplex

LANDSCAPE ARCHITECTS
Site Concepts

PROJECT DATE
2004 – 2007

11.01 RAGHULEELA MALL

The brief was to create an IT building combined with a mall that would include all the elements of a shopping paradise. The requirement specification spanned an atrium, a multiplex, banquet halls with separate entrances, an entertainment zone, a food court, 3 speciality restaurants and 2 basements for car parking – one for the IT workforce and one for mall patrons. A location opposite Vashi station, Mumbai was selected for development. The structure consists of a 7,00,000 sft area, consisting of 4 floors of shopping mall with the remaining designated as office space for IT ventures. The shopping mall sits on 1,00,000 sft with 40,000 sft area being assigned to the main atrium located at the centre of the base and 10,000 sft area split into disparate sections to create a modular design and to create a sense of space while optimally allocating space to the retail outlets within. The main atrium is covered by a modernistic conical glass skylight, which greets the visitor with a spectacular view from the entrance.

11.01 RAGHULEELA MALL

The central glass roof covering is made out of a double-layered 5mm + 5mm laminated glass with a 0.5mm layer of PVB sandwiched between the two to make it energy efficient. The glass structure is built on steel lattices implementing tension and compression rods. The façade materials are Ikon brown granite, chosen to complement the colours of the surrounding environment. Aluminium composite panels have been used because they are light weight and easy to install. Glass has been used to allow natural light to flood the spacious open foyer. The façade structures are light-weight elements stiffened with steel studs, thermo purlin structures, steel, glass and aluminium glass. The variety of interior materials has been carefully selected. The main themes were durability, elegance, warmth and light tones. Raghuleela Mall is imbued with a sense of delight in each detail, offering visitors an enchanting journey. It aims to create a destination of urban cultural experience for residents rather than simply emphasising business functions.

RAGHULEELA
RAGHULEELA
BIG BAZAAR

RAGHULEELA
Welcome to a
Unique Shopping
Experience
Ghar ka har
Samaan
kam daam
mein
BIG BAZAAR

SITE PLAN

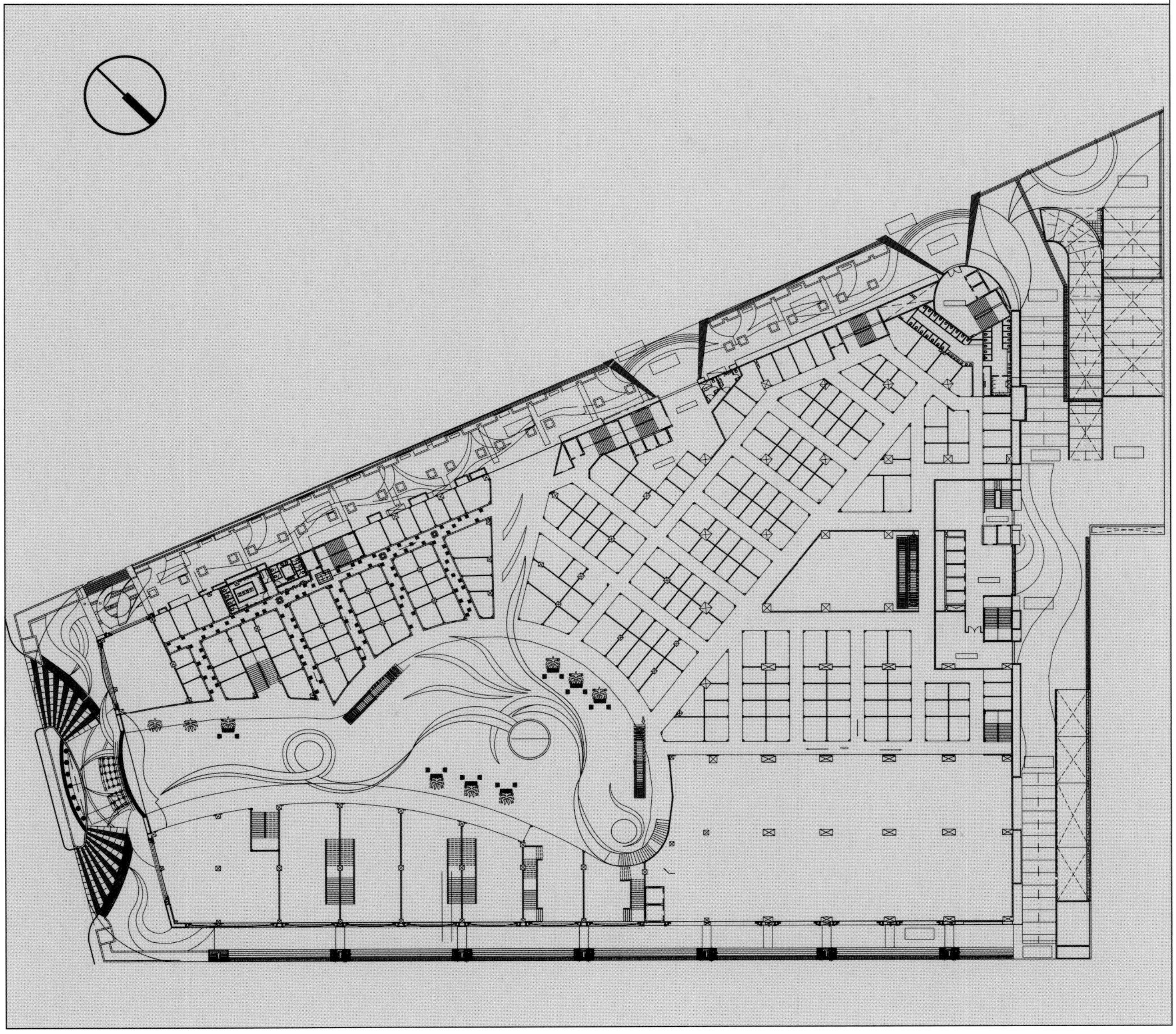

Given the variety of functional structures within the same framework, placing supporting columns within the structures presented a unique challenge. The shopping zone followed a different axis vis-à-vis the IT space. Consequently, the columns had to be rotated in the lower floors. Additionally, the columns had to be placed so as to not create a hindrance to accommodating shop spaces on the lower floors. Furthermore, a theatre had to be installed within the same grid. Eventually, a post-tension system was used which allowed for larger grids easing the planning work. Cantilevers had to be used to keep the main atrium free of columns. Prestressed beams were used to aid the process. The other challenge was the execution of the conical glass skylight within budget constraints. A technique called "Ball and Socket" was used where the glass pieces and the supporting steel structure were prefabricated. Laminated glass was used for strength and stability and to cut down on sun glare, thereby reducing cooling needs and making the structure energy efficient.

CLIENT
Shirazi Mosque

CATEGORY
Mosque

LOCATION
Imamwada, Mumbai

PRINCIPAL ARCHITECT
Reza Kabul

CONTRACTORS
Shafi Constructions

PROJECT DATE
2003 – 2007

11.02 SHIRAZI MOSQUE

Constructed by an Iranian trader over a century ago, the Shirazi Mosque restoration project was both, a challenge and an opportunity for Reza. The mosque's entrance, scaling 4 stories, opens onto a landscaped courtyard that adorns a water pond, *hauz*. The mosque itself, constructed primarily with rubble masonry and lime mortar, is elevated on a 4 ft plinth. The roof is built with wooden trusses and Mangalore tiles. The restoration started by addressing the key structural concerns – the foundation, walls and the roof. On review, Reza and his team found major structural cracks in the 2.6 ft thick load-bearing walls of the main structure of the mosque. Furthermore, the roof was in a dilapidated state showing high probability of collapsing in the near future. Water had seeped through the damaged roof, severely eroding the structure. The cracks extended to the *hauz* – a structure filled with water for the devotees to purify themselves prior to entering the Mosque. The cracks allowed drainage water to seep into the *hauz*, making it unusable. After repairing and water-proofing the roof and the walls, finishing of the interiors was done by cladding the walls with Onyx and a band of granite with inlays of *surah* (verses from the Quran). A fresh water source was added and the fountain adorning the *hauz* was restored to working order. Additional blue tiles were added to enhance the *hauz's* intrinsic beauty.

11.02 SHIRAZI MOSQUE

Next, Reza and his team tackled the restoration of the *mehraab* – a structure situated in the mosque facing the house of God in Mecca – the Kaba. The *mehraab* was clad with mosaic tiles imported from Iran with inlays of the *surah*. The interior was embellished by a 3-tier crystal chandelier, also brought in from Iran along with Persian carpets. The external façade, too, was adorned with Iranian tiles. Finally, the minarets and main gate were restored. The minarets are the tallest structures in the Mosque. Traditionally used for calls to prayer, *azaan*, the minarets now serve an aesthetic purpose since *azaan* is now dispensed via loud speakers fitted atop the minarets. The main gate – a grand 80 ft tall structure, was renovated with a cladding of Iranian tiles. The restoration process took 4 years primarily due to the fact that the materials were being imported from Iran.

CONCEPT SKETCHES

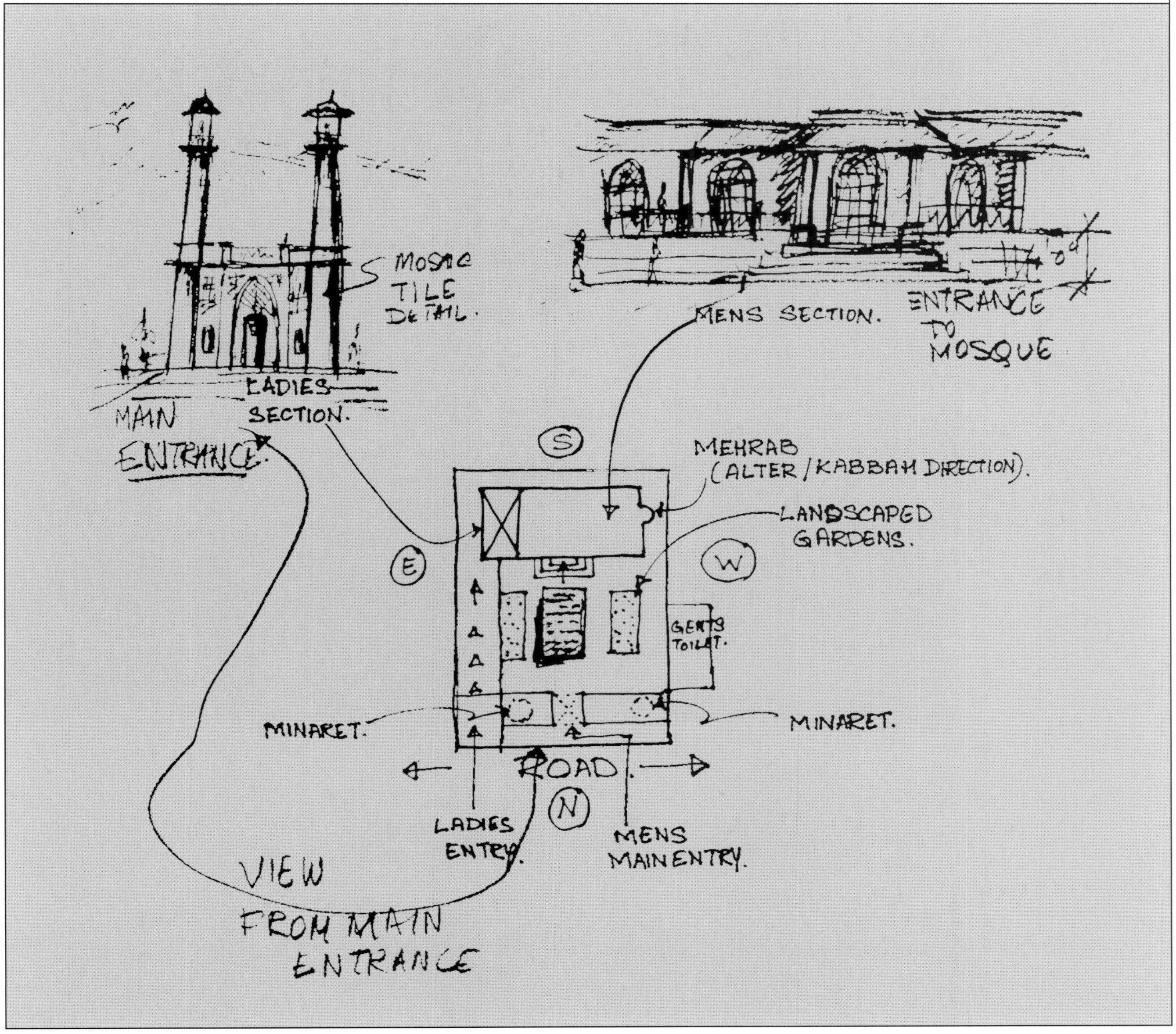

When Reza took up the assignment, little did he know how arduous a task it would be. The Mosque was significantly damaged. The fact that it was declared a heritage structure, prohibited rebuilding parts of the structure. Consequently the only option was to repair and fortify as much of the existing structure as was possible and replace only that, which was damaged beyond repair. Furthermore, being a place of prayer, the Mosque had to continue serving its function. Consequently, every day, the Mosque had to be cleaned an hour before prayers commenced, which meant a cessation of restoration functions. The work also had to be ceased during *Ramzaan*. Monsoons, too, caused delays in implementation work. Another key challenge was to carry out the restoration using traditional materials, since the existing walls were made of lime stone and brick as opposed to modern materials like cement and mortar. Consequently, restoration had to be carried out using traditional means and retain the originality of the structure while using modern techniques.

FIRM NAME
P G Patki Architects Pvt Ltd

ADDRESS
First Floor, Calcot House
8, Tamarind Lane
Opp St Thomas Church, Fort
Mumbai 400001
Maharashtra

CONTACT
Tel: +91 22 61408888, +91 22 22049182

There is no convention to the mind; it is a continuous stream of ideas and possibilities flowing, running to be captured and translated. It is what makes for the evolution of the world]

12 S P PATKI

Born in Mumbai, S P Patki completed his schooling from Doon School, Dehradun. He went on to study architecture at the J J School of Architecture, Mumbai. He attributes his strong learning foundation to his early days at his father's firm. "School is but where the skeleton of architecture is structured, but the seed is nurtured and nourished outside this realm where the persevering mind may initially struggle only to flourish and bloom in the expanse of the real world to bring out ones creativity. This is where one embarks and covers real ground based on one's discipline, imagination and merit." He took over the reins of P G Patki Architects Pvt Ltd, after his father, guru and mentor P G Patki passed away. The firm is involved in numerous successful projects encompassing luxury hotels & resorts, hospitals, residential & commercial complexes, IT parks and townships. Patki recognizes that the demands and the challenges of the industry have widened the role, scope and responsibilities of architects and architectural companies. It is no longer only about creative flair, design and construction. There is a pressing and exacting need to be abreast and in-sync with other areas, which are an integral part of the field and go hand-in-hand; a key to competitiveness and survival. A project is not just about design and construction, but goes beyond the ambit to engage a host of other parameters that include dealing with various agencies, municipal laws, marketing, optimum space planning, finance, building material & technology and research & development. An additional dimension is that of providing efficiency, functionality and comprehensive solutions without compromising on the basic tenets and needs. He reiterates, "An architect's role today is a balancing act where detail, character and fundamentals are not compromised and where the structure reflects the mark of the individual; the soul behind it."

CLIENT
Oberoi Hotels

CATEGORY
Luxury Hotel

LOCATION
Agra, Uttar Pradesh

PRINCIPAL ARCHITECT
S P Patki

DESIGN TEAM
Harshad Piparia

STRUCTURAL, MECHANICAL & ELECTRICAL, HVAC / PLUMBING
Rajani Associates
Spectral Services Consultants

CONTRACTORS
Oberoi McAlpine India Ltd

LANDSCAPE ARCHITECTS
Bensley Design Studio

PROJECT DATE
1997 – 2000

12.01 THE OBEROI AMARVILAS

There can, perhaps, be no greater challenge than designing a structure in the shadows of the Taj Mahal. The architectural concept for The Oberoi Amarvilas is an adaptation of the Andulesean Style of Architecture reminiscent of the Ottoman empire of the Turks. This is reflected in the styling of the flat domes of the buildings, the design of the arches and the fenestration embellishment details. The landscape and overall site development is styled to reflect the sensibilities of Mughal Gardens. Private terraces attached to the guest rooms overlooking the Taj Mahal were created by stepping back the structure at three different levels, marking alternate floors. The top guest floor is designed to have all suites with private terraces and bathrooms facing the Taj Mahal. Floor-to-ceiling windows in the lounges, bars, restaurants and some of the spa suites, offer the guests an unparalleled view of the ethereal translucence of the Taj. The dining areas are located at the lowest level of the contour. This level also includes the health club. Mughal styled gardens and a swimming pool conceptualized on traditional stepped wells have been engineered on the lower contours.

12.01 THE OBEROI AMARVILAS

The appearance of the hotel seems to change with the subtle nuances of the light and the sky. The experience carries through as one walks down the elaborate grand staircase into the lower terraces and then further down into the open colonnaded porticos with their sunken gardens and pool. At dusk, this place becomes a magical land. You'll definitely hear a muezzin in the distance, his plaintive tones rising, falling and echoing off the stone walls. One may also hear the harsh cry of a peacock among the dark silhouettes of crows flying overhead. The visual impact one experiences when one walks through the water-scaped gardens into the main lobby is accentuated by its enormous volume capped with the delicately designed dome and framing of the Taj Mahal by its central arches. With the ever present sounds of gurgling water and the backdrop of the Taj Mahal, it is easy to forget the real world in this eternal abode.

SITE PLAN

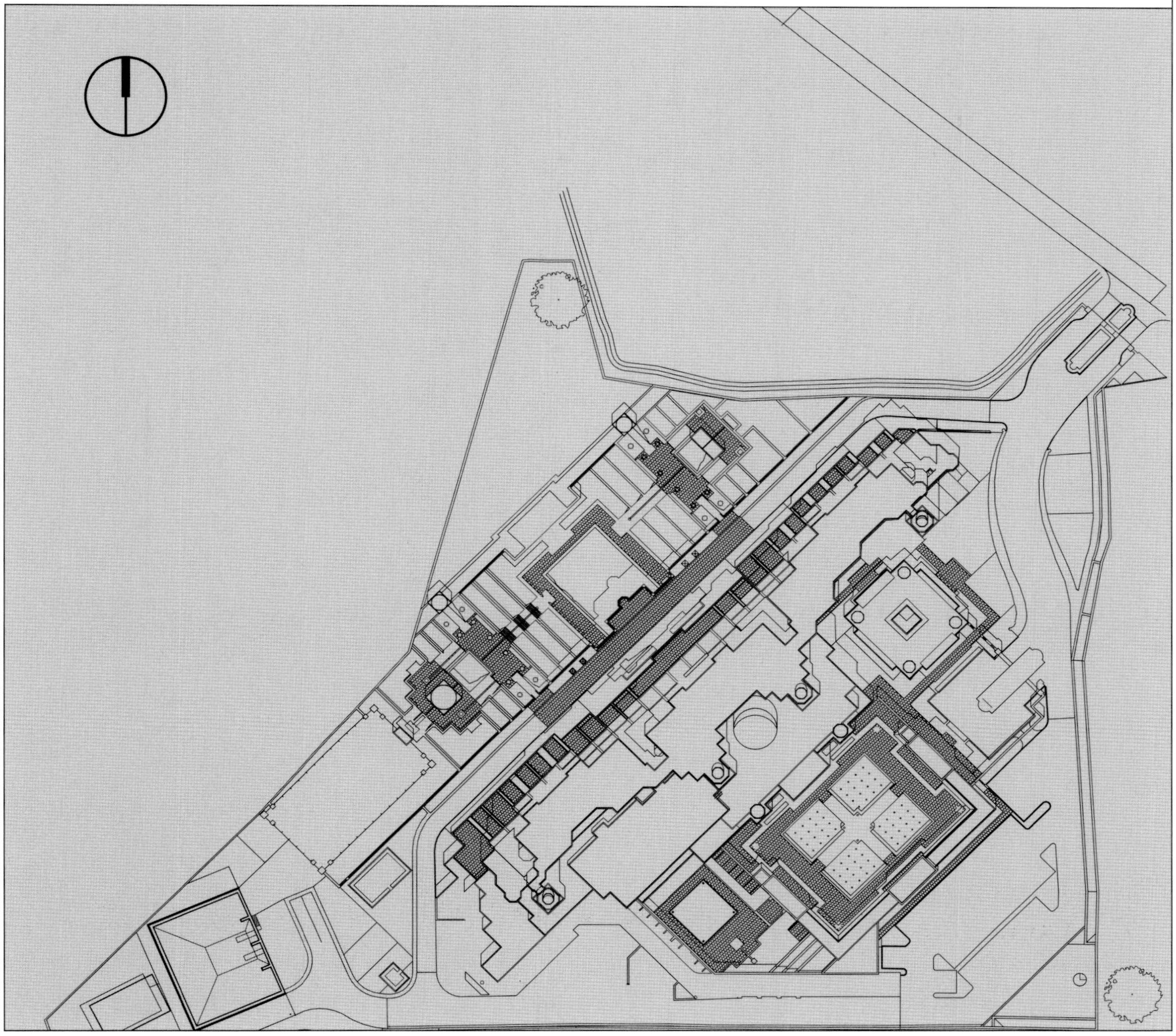

Private vehicular movement has been restricted to the entrance area to provide the guest with a walk-through experience of the Mughal Garden with water bodies, channels, colonnades and pavilions. The fire tender movement has been well identified with hard paving all around the building in the form of terraces and ramps to blend-in with the Mughal Garden concept. All the modern amenities are provided with deep consideration to the green practices especially in house-keeping management, and through the use of minimal pollution propane gas. The site was heavily contoured. While some might see this as a design hindrance, the architect saw this as an opportunity. Confining the design program within the framework of regulations and adhering to the height restriction was a challenge in itself that was to be ingeniously used to conceptualize and create interesting public spaces along with five levels of guest room floors.

CLIENT
Osho International

CATEGORY
Meditation Centre

LOCATION
Pune, Maharashtra

PRINCIPAL ARCHITECT
S P Patki

DESIGN TEAM
Praveen Thakur

STRUCTURAL, MECHANICAL & ELECTRICAL
Rajani Associates
Spectral Services Consultants

LANDSCAPE ARCHITECTS
P G Patki Architects

CONTRACTORS
Semb Corp Infrastructure (India) Pvt Ltd

PROJECT DATE
1997 – 2001

12.02 OSHO COMMUNE

The Osho International Foundation wanted a large meditation resort at the Koregaon Park in Pune. The primary function of this complex was to provide a meditation hall with one single floor space of 25,000 sft as the hall area. It also has a large kitchen which can cater to about 4,000 people at a time. The foremost challenge and focus was to create a comprehensive community centre within a single complex on a narrow long plot to achieve the varied objectives and program set by the commune. This essentially consisted of a large meditation hall, a separate structure dedicated to guests, dining areas and a main community kitchen. Skillful arrangement of elements and a combination of Italian marble makes this space the most pivotal and integral part of the overall complex.

12.02 OSHO COMMUNE

The entrance to the meditation hall at the upper level is punctuated with a sanitized foyer that leads to the hall. It is an essential section of the community centre, which has been carefully structured. Due care was taken at the planning stage to separate the entries and yet use the common spaces to achieve the desired integration between the functions. In order to provide maximum and optimum space, the meditation hall has been designed with a pyramidal roof resting on only four columns roughly 100 ft apart, thus providing a virtually cclumn free square base of 25,000 sft. The meditation hall's ceiling is treated with acoustical boards so that there is no echo or resonance. A diffused lighting technique has been used to enhance the ambient light. The overall restriction in colour has been dutifully adhered to and a variation in material, texture and finish has been used to provide contrast and evoke a non-traditional, non-conformist quality as a design response to the teachings of Osho. The restraint from sharp colours and contrasts lend a warm, soothing, soft ambience and expression; a tone of spirituality.

SITE PLAN

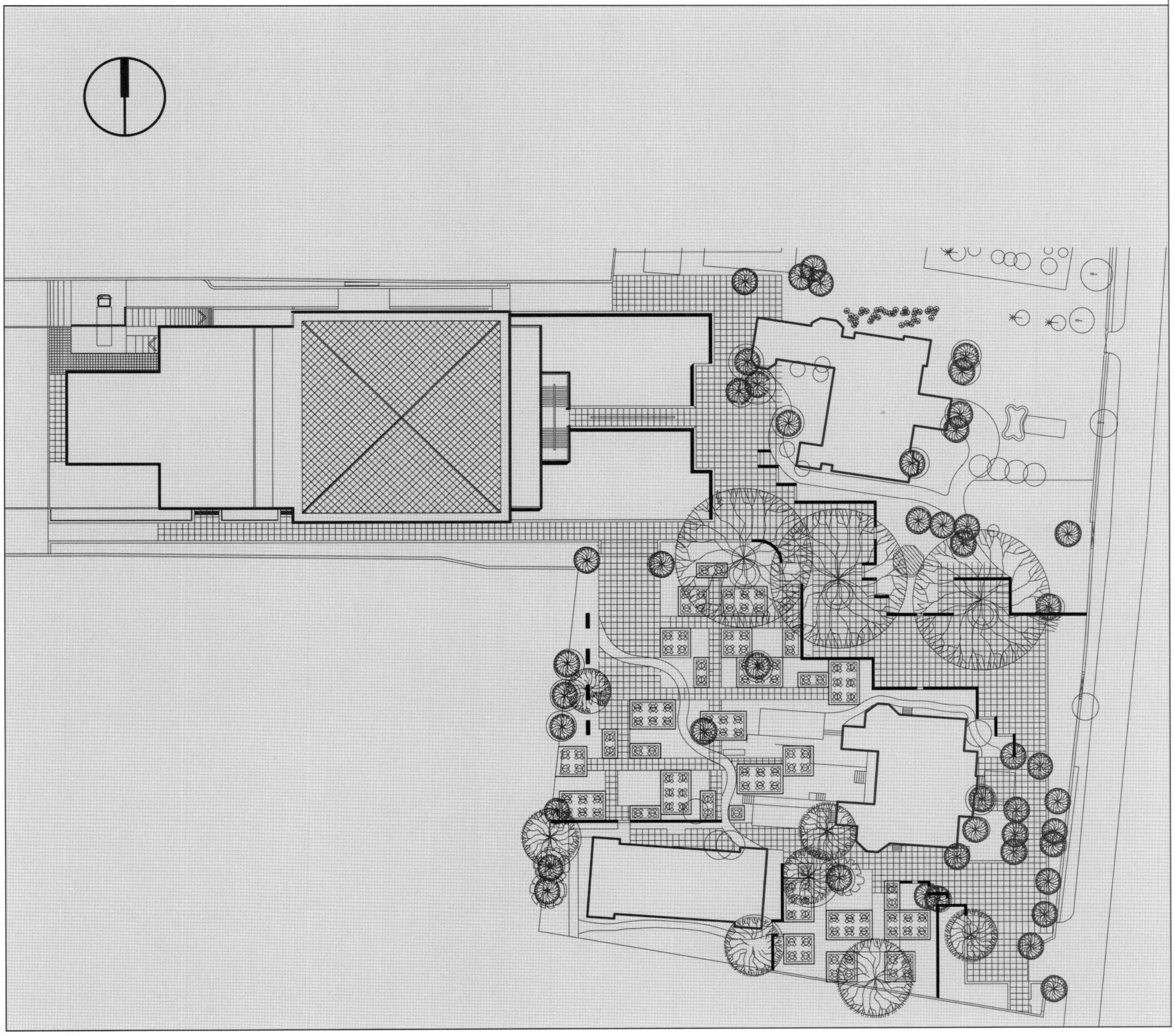

Apart from the shades of black for building surfaces and blue glass, the use of other colours is brief and sparse. Granite stone is used widely in the form of polished slabs, thick flamed slabs, dressed blocks for steps and kerbs. In combination, for the paving and plazas, dull black *cudappah* slabs of meter by meter grid with dressed granite kerbs have been used. Landscaped screen walls have been clad with layers of *cudappah* stacked with the edge side exposed. Black metal surfaces have been extensively used and the pyramid roof is clad with black coated aluminium sheets. The building dedicated to guests demanded a rigid disciplined grid, which has been carried through the enormous community kitchen in keeping with the needs of the commune.

FIRM NAME
Sanjay Puri Architects Pvt Ltd

ADDRESS
20 Famous Studio Lane
Off Dr E Moses Road
Mahalaxmi, Mumbai 400011
Maharashtra

CONTACT
Tel: +91 22 24965840 / 41 / 42/ 43 / 44
www.sanjaypuriarchitects.com

My work strives to evolve innovative design solutions that are contextual and sustainable and create spaces that are exhilarating to experience while being functional]

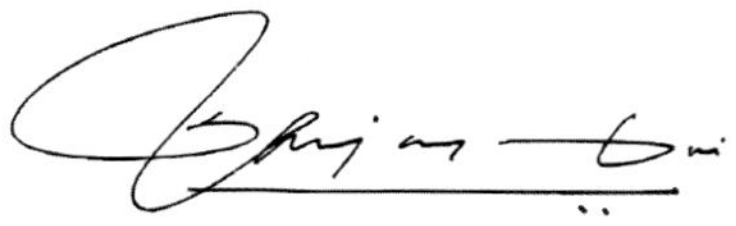

13 SANJAY PURI

After graduating from Mayo College, Sanjay Puri pursued his studies in architecture at the Academy of Architecture (Rachna Sansad), Mumbai to create his destiny. Throughout the 5 years of his studies in architecture, Sanjay worked with the now famous Hafeez Contractor as a junior architect. His first major architectural work was commissioned by Apar Ltd, to design the interiors for of the Dharmsinh Desai Institute of Technology in Nadiad, which included the institute's library, the computer lab and the renovation work on the entire building. A 54-acre township in Vasai for Sheth Developers was the milestone project, which encouraged Sanjay, then 27, to start his own firm, Sanjay Puri Architects Pvt Ltd in 1992. To date, his company has won over 30 awards, including an international award – the Architectural Review MIPIM award, 5 from the Indian Institute of Architects and 6 from the Indian Institute of Interior Designers. The company's work has been extensively featured in both national and international magazines with over 20 international publications featuring their projects in 2008 alone. Having already completed over 400 projects, the company is currently involved in over 200 projects including townships, hotels, residential and corporate office buildings, retail malls, institutes, clubs and schools. A recent survey by MIRVAC, citing the 47 most exciting architectural projects being built in the UAE, included two buildings, Synergy and ETA hotel in Dubai designed by Sanjay Puri Architects.

CLIENT
Amby Valley Lake Sahara City, Sahara Group

CATEGORY
Leisure Centre

LOCATION
Lonavala, Maharashtra

PRINCIPAL ARCHITECT
Sanjay Puri

STRUCTURAL, HVAC & UTILITIES

D E G Consultants

CONTRACTORS
Interdecor

LANDSCAPE ARCHITECTS
Sanjay Puri

PROJECT DATE
July 2005 – December 2005

13.01 AMBY VALLEY LEISURE CENTRE

The Sahara Group wanted to develop a 4,921 sft leisure centre with plenty of lounge areas, cafeteria, souvenir shop, badminton court, table tennis room, squash court, mother care room, siesta room and children's room among others, in an area abundant with natural resources, which needed to be utilized imaginatively. Sanjay decided to delineate the entire unit into several platforms of varying heights. Therefore, each section like the cafeteria, library, office, lounge and the Internet café, is separated only by ground level. The beautiful natural surroundings are visible from each space within the building. Floating panels in the ceiling that are linear and trapezoidal in shape and suspended at varying levels enhance the winding movement of the low wood partitions. The only side of the internal volume with a high blank wall is rendered sculptural by creating a layered effect with trapezoidal planes of varying heights and depths that are enhanced by reflective lighting. The irregular-shaped linear platforms in white sandstone, with rising and falling wood partition; linear trapezoidal floating ceiling panels and layered walls together create an abstract sculptural feel. This layout allows uninterrupted views of the exterior landscape with gardens and hills. In addition, the large landscaped garden adjacent to the building is visible through the 24 ft high wood and glass exterior skin; the internal lounge platforms of varying height extend out into the landscaped foreground creating continuity between the interior and exterior.

13.01 AMBY VALLEY LEISURE CENTRE

The ceiling roof with AC ducts, structural system and electric cable trays painted in black, floating trapezoidal panels in wood and shades of white, create a sculptural effect. The wood partitions allow privacy to the lounge areas and create space for display, an internet café and a library within, allowing the interior space to be perceived in entirety. The rear wall is fragmented into a series of panels accentuated by reflected light that renders it as a sculptural backdrop. Each level is bound by wood partitions that change the direction in plan and vary in height and thickness simultaneously creating a rhythm and sculptural effect. In conclusion, the Amby Valley project has gained instant recognition as a work of creative genius. The project is famous for its inspirational design which encourages cohabiting peacefully with nature functionally and creatively.

SITE PLAN

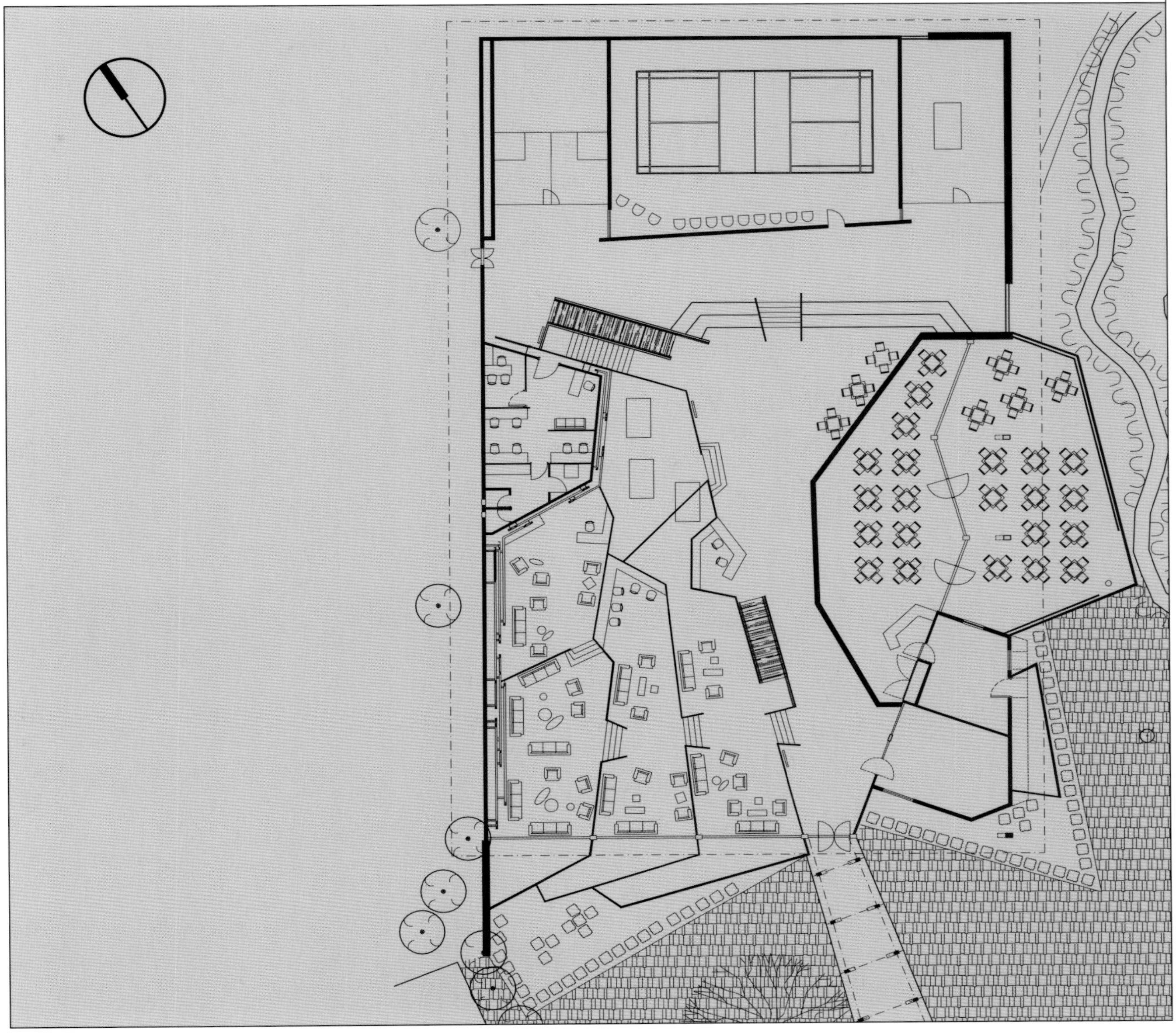

When this project was awarded to Sanjay Puri Architects, they were informed that the main steel portal frame for the building had already been ordered. Therefore, they had the restriction of designing within a preconceived rectangular framework. Yet, when one perceives the final built form, this is not apparent even slightly, since they wove the glass wood skin of the building in and out of the rectangular frame, angling façades and creating interesting interiors as well as exteriors. The other dominant challenge was the restricted time frame. The project had to be completed within 6 months and they were given only a week to finalize all designs, issue working drawings and appoint contractors and commence work within a restricted budget. The entire design was completed and work commenced within a week. Being a sculptural space, a considerable amount of design was done on site simultaneously during construction work.

CLIENT
Kalapatru Group of Companies

CATEGORY
Residential Complex

LOCATION
Mumbai, Maharashtra

PRINCIPAL ARCHITECT
Sanjay Puri

DESIGN TEAM
Kulin Dhruva
Hetal Mehta

STRUCTURAL, MECHANICAL & ELECTRICAL
Vakil Mehta Sheth
M W H
Design Bureau

LANDSCAPE ARCHITECT
Ravi Purandare

HVAC
Rumi Bharucha Consulting Engineer

PROJECT DATE
2005 – 2007

13.02 KALPATARU HORIZON

Kalpataru Horizon, Worli, is a premium residential complex comprising of 30 storeyed twin towers. The size of the complex is approximately 2,00,000 sft and includes approximately three acres of land. The complex has been designed to give each flat an uninterrupted view of the beautiful Arabian Sea. There are 3 (1,800 sft) and 4 (3,500 sft) bedroom apartments and penthouses. The residential complex has a podium car park with a garden. The flats begin at 130 ft, giving each flat owner a sense of space and a chance to view the sea without any interruptions. The biggest challenge that the architects faced in this project was to provide unrestricted sea view to all the rooms including the kitchen in all the apartments. The building towers are far away from the sea with numerous low rise buildings in between, which is the reason why the first floor had to be built at 130 ft.

13.02 KALPATARU HORIZON

The recreational facilities include a curvilinear clubhouse spread over 24,000 sft, a gymnasium, a spacious party lounge, indoor game room, squash court, steam room, massage room, rooftop swimming pool in each tower and ample car parking. The swimming pools in both the towers have been thoughtfully constructed on the top floors with a deck, which gives the pool area privacy and an unrestricted private view of the sea. Large 20 ft high skylit entrance lobbies lead one into the buildings. At the building entrance, a huge expanse has been constructed, which invites natural light during daytime. This section of the complex is lit by sunlight only, making it a nature lover's delight.

FLOOR PLAN

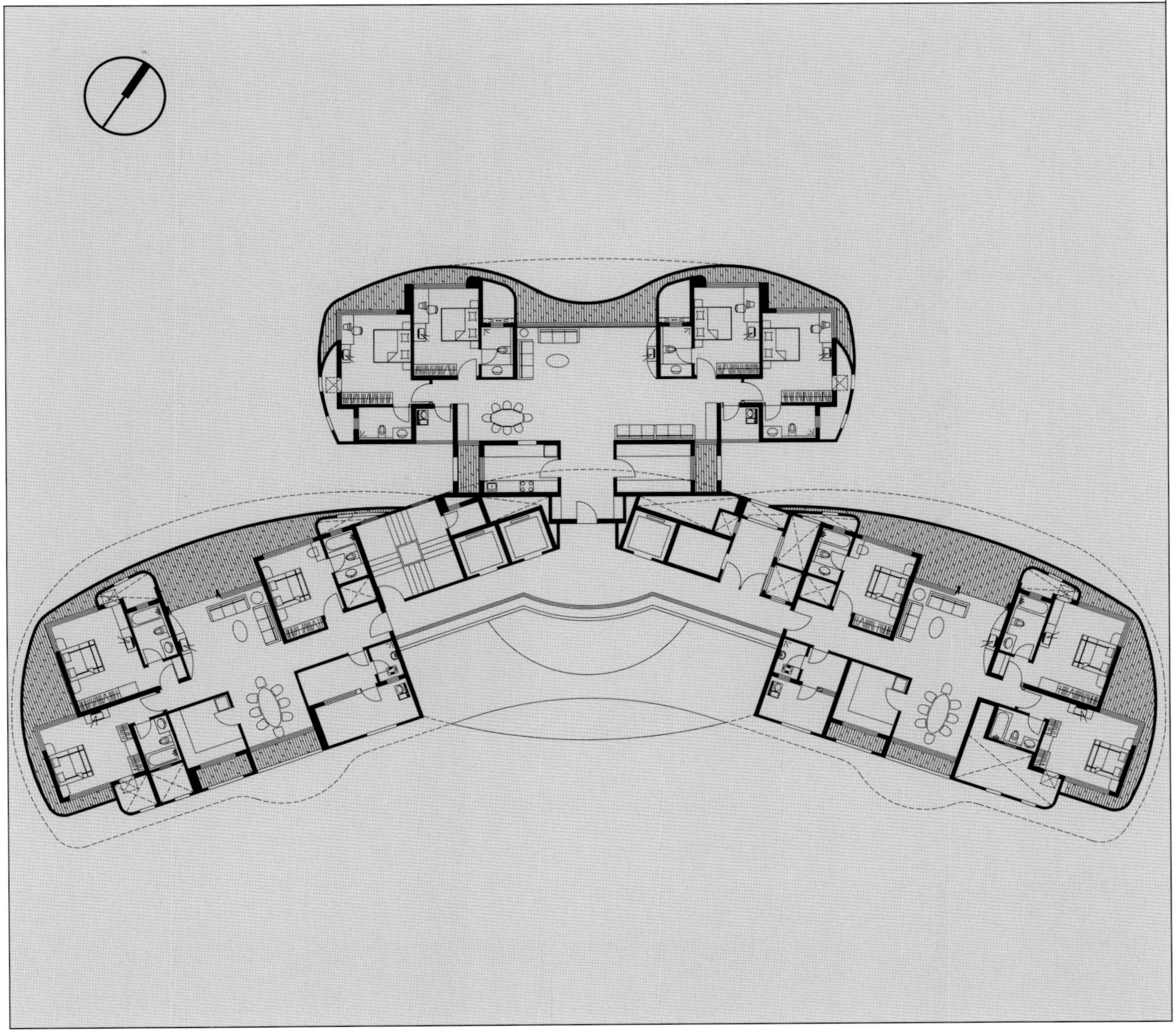

Although the architects had proposed to build a single tower in the long narrow plot to maximize on the open spaces within the site, the developers insisted on two towers. The challenge here was to build two towers that did not overlook each other and still orient all the apartments, three on each floor, towards the sea view, which was available across the length of the plot. The two towers are, therefore, located at the extreme ends of the plot to maximize the garden area between them. According to the prevalent rules, the area between the ground and the elevated height coul not be used for any functional purpose except parking. The design provides for sufficient parking within a single large podium at the ground floor itself. The empty space thus had to be an integral part of the design of the built form. This was done in a composition of glass bricks and textured walls that create a simple yet interesting base for the building above and is integrated holistically in the building.

FIRM NAME
Shashi Prabhu & Associates

ADDRESS
Wankhade Stadium
North Stand, C Block
D Road, Churchgate
Mumbai 400020
Maharashtra

CONTACT
Tel: +91 22 22811739 / 4931 / 3599

In continuous improvement is success and in stagnation is death]

14 SHASHI PRABHU

Shashi Prabhu spent his formative years in Mumbai as a Shivaji Park resident. After completing his schooling, he joined the R A Poddar College of Commerce following which, he joined the Bandra School of Architecture (now Raheja College of Architecture). After graduating in 1967, he decided to venture out on his own. Shashi's milestone project arrived with a request from Professor M V Changadkar, a professor of English at R A Poddar College and the Joint Honorary Secretary of the Bombay Cricket Association. They asked Shashi to design the Garware Club House for MCA, at a newly acquired ground in Churchgate, Mumbai. His next impressive project was to design Wankhede Stadium at a tender age 26. The architect's tryst with designing health care structures began in 1977. His first structure was a hospital designed for Thane Corporation, which was followed by several others in Pimpri, Chinchwad with the most prominent being Lilavati in Mumbai. He is currently proud to be associated with the latest Sir Harkishandas Hospital, Mumbai, promoted by Reliance Industries with many others in the pipeline. His keen insight into the dynamics of health care structures is undeniable and well-recognized. Since its inception, Shashi Prabhu & Associates has grown substantially. With over a 100 employees, most of them experienced architects, the company has grown from strength to strength. Shashi Prabhu's sons, Amol and Atul are part of the company and contribute significantly with their design, engineering, project management and financial analysis skill set. The company undertakes projects on turnkey basis, which they believe will be the future trend.

CLIENT
Director of Sports & Youth Services
Government of Maharashtra

CATEGORY
Government Sports Complex

LOCATION
Pune, Maharashtra

PRINCIPAL ARCHITECT
Shashi Prabhu & Associates

DESIGN TEAM
Amol Prabhu
Atul Prabhu
Anand Bhave
Santosh Yadav
Anup Vinekar

STRUCTURAL, MECHANICAL & ELECTRICAL
Frichman Prabhu India Pvt Ltd
Jayant Pathak

CONTRACTORS
B G Shirke Const Tech Pvt Ltd

LANDSCAPE ARCHITECTS
Gauresh Chandavarkar

HVAC
Deepak Inamdar

PROJECT DATE
2007 – 2008

14.01 SHIVAJI CHHATRAPATI SPORTS CITY

In 1992-93, the then Chief Minister of Maharashtra, decided to develop a sports facility on a 150 acre plot on the outskirts of Pune at Balewadi. This herculean task was assigned to Shashi Prabhu & Architects. While the execution was in progress, it was decided to conduct the National Games in 1994. When the venue was chosen for the Common Wealth Youth Games (CYG), Shashi Prabhu participated in a competition held to determine who the project would be awarded to. He won and was awarded the assignment to restore and create additional facilities for CYG. The regulations laid out by CYG were stringent with respect to dimensions, lighting arrangements, sports equipment, floorings and protocols for conducting of games. With stringent norms and numerous interests vested in the structure, the architects knew they had a challenge that would put his skills to the test. The biggest challenge was the time frame. The dates for the CYG event had been announced. Traffic co-ordination, security, water supply, power generation and landscaping required managing multiple service providers, which proved to be a complex venture. Furthermore, with demands from the Federation to match International standards, the estimated 196 crore cost was raised to 355 crores.

Modern construction materials comprising of aluminium composite panels and glass were judicially used in constructing the structures. The resulting structure, completed in August of 2008, is a world class monument. With 13 sport facilities, 280 rooms to accommodate 500 participants and a 400 room deluxe hotel, the structure is equipped for world championships.

badminton

get set go!
TABLE TENNIS

SITE PLAN

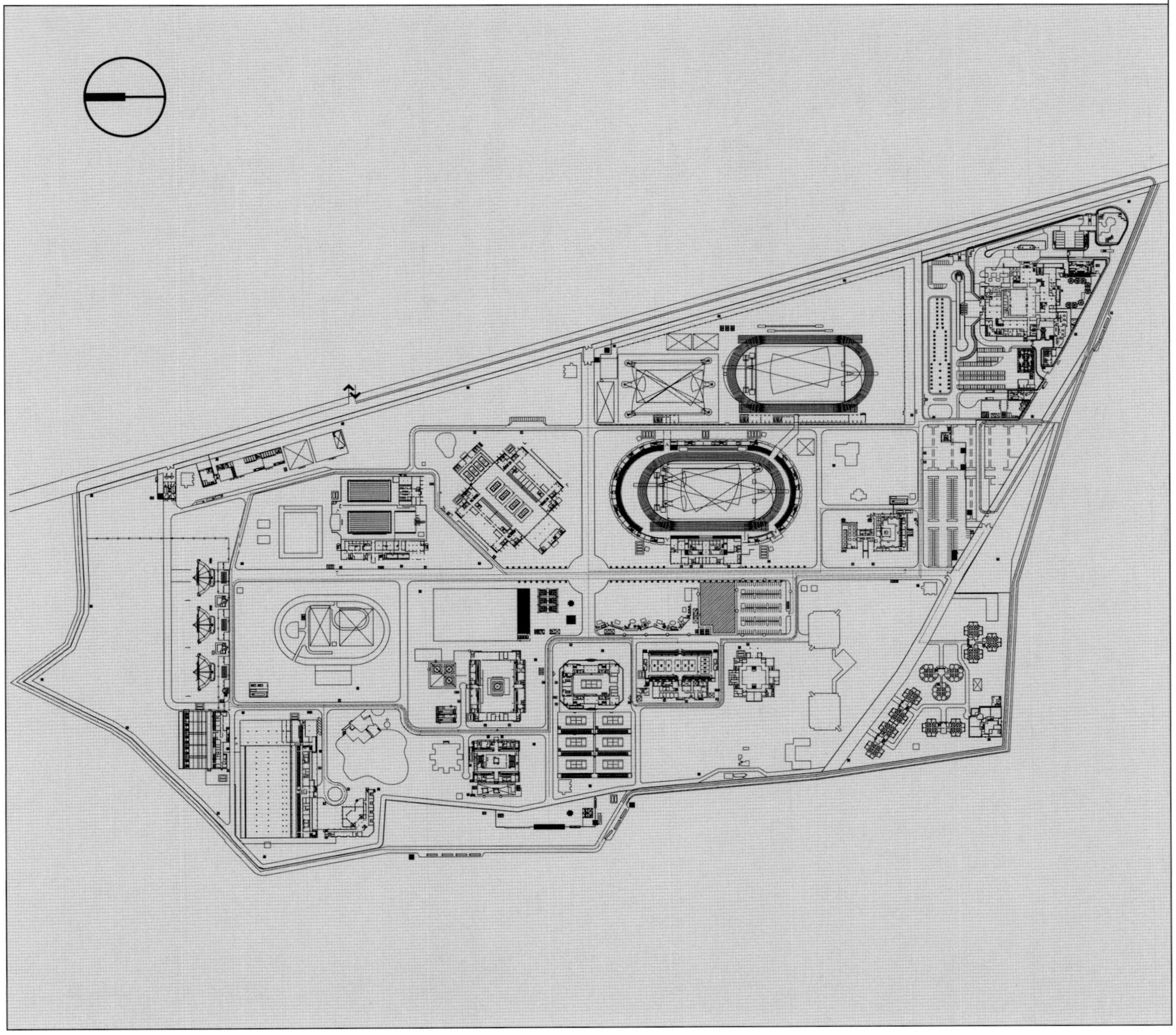

The structure is home to athletics, badminton, boxing, volleyball, table tennis, wrestling, shooting, cycling and swimming. With 13 different sports facilities within the same structure, the developmental challenge was multifaceted. Issues were addressed by visualizing the facilities as an integrated unit. The architects had to ensure that despite the multitude of sub-units, the structure was combined in aesthetic harmony. An additional challenge came from the labour faction. However, despite the challenges, deadlines were met and the Common Youth Games were successfully conducted in Oct 2008.

LILAVATI HOSPITA

CLIENT
Lilavati Medical Trust

CATEGORY
Healthcare

LOCATION
Mumbai, Maharashtra

PRINCIPAL ARCHITECT
Shashi Prabhu

DESIGN TEAM
Suhas Sahani

STRUCTURAL, MECHANICAL & ELECTRICAL
Satish Dhupelia
Shah Vidyut Electricals

CONTRACTORS
Shapoorji Pallonji

PROJECT DATE
1990 – 1992

14.02 LILAVATI HOSPITAL

Lilavati Hospital is a proud landmark on the health care map of Mumbai. The hospital has been set up by late Shri Kirtilal Mehta, in fond memory of his wife, on a plot of 2 acres at Bandra Reclamation. The development guidelines stipulated for a charitable hospital, dedicated to health care with a bed capacity of 300. Special care has been given to the three main functional areas of the hospital – the emergency care facility, the OPD and the inpatients. A Floor Space Program played a significant role in the design of the emergency care department. Shashi derives pride in the fact that this department has a plan like none-other and equipped with 3rd generation technology. The location and department's connectivity with the pathology & radiology department has been planned with such efficiency that a patient can be diagnosed in a couple of minutes.

14.02 LILAVATI HOSPITAL

A detailed research was conducted to study several hospitals abroad and within the country to understand their functional dynamics before sitting down on the drawing board. The architects took educated and ingenious decisions to create a second-to-none structure dedicated to health care, resulting in Lilavati being a hospital with 17 operation theatres, 30 speciality OPDs and 300 beds served by a staff of 3,000 people working 24/7 with ease and efficiency. Typical upper floors of the hospital are based on an L-shaped plan, with service areas in the middle and patients recovery rooms placed on either side of the corridors. A large lounge area has been placed at the entrance for visitors at ground floor level, as well as on every floor with a capacity to seat 70 visitors. Colours are used thoughtfully in this project. The children's ward is bright and cheerful with wall paintings, keeping the atmosphere lively. Green is used in the operation theatre for a soothing effect.

GROUND FLOOR PLAN

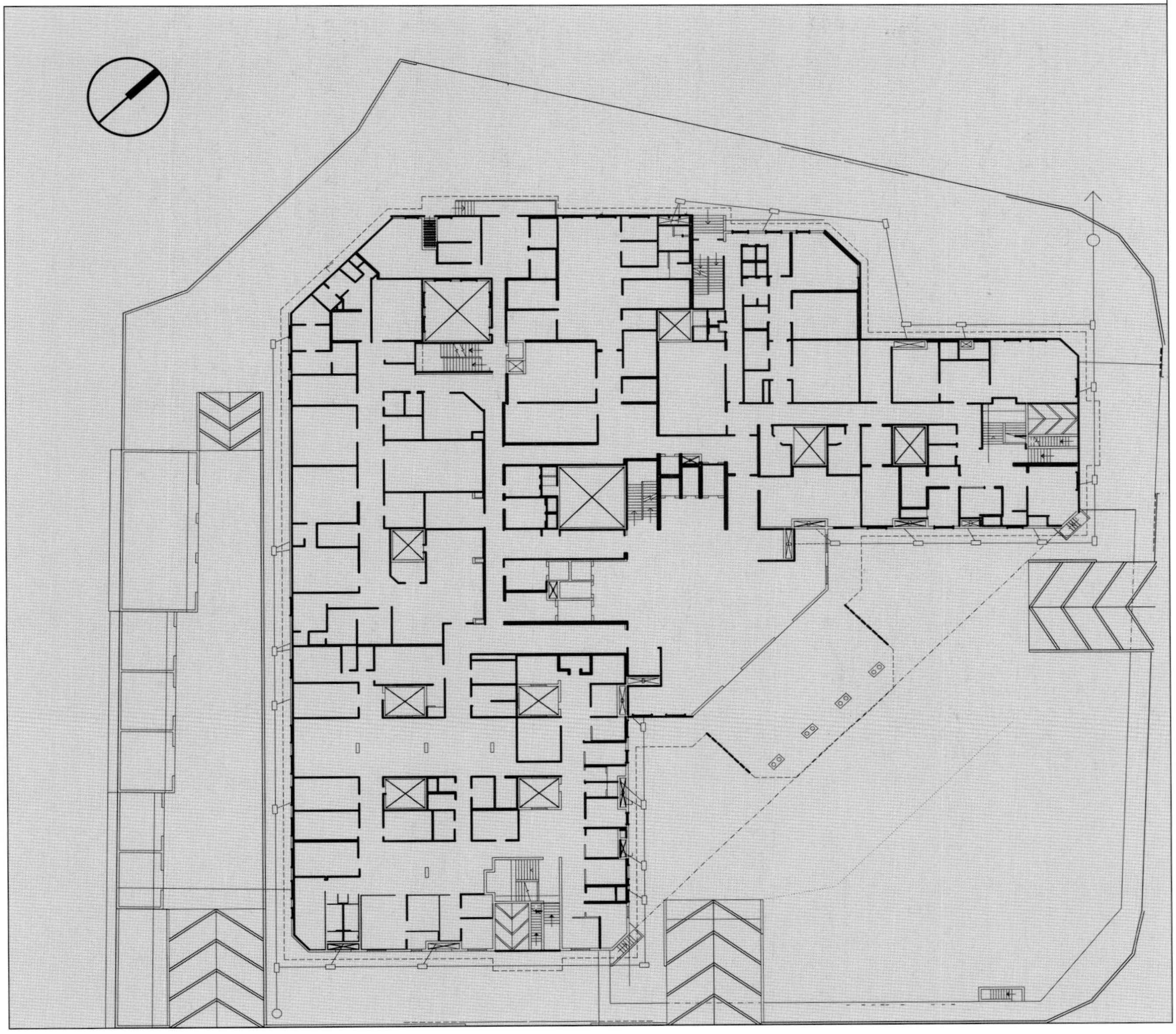

The challenge in designing this structure was to ensure that each department received optimal utility and services based on its unique requirements. A Floor Space Program (FSP) was finalized along with doctors, surgeons & nursing staff. Every square foot area of the plan was discussed and the basis of its allocation justified. Key parameters to such detailed planning were the areas functional responsibility and its adjacency to dependent departments. Planning of the hospital has been done on the basis of FSP, wherein every square feet of constructed area has utility as per the design program and justified in terms of utility and viability in relation to the total economics of hospital to achieve rapid turnaround times leading to more rooms for new patients due to efficient discharge of recovered patients.

FIRM NAME
DSP Design Associates

ADDRESS
5th Floor, Rahimtoola House
7 Homji Street,
Fort, Mumbai 400001
Maharashtra

CONTACT
Tel: +91 22 22651021
www.dspdesign.co.in

DSP Design Associates believes in architecture that is sustainable and responsive to social and economic parameters]

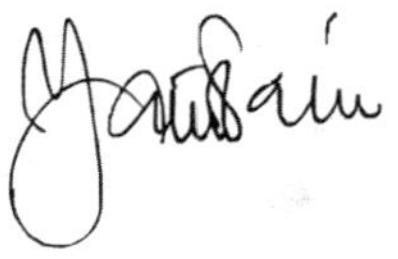

15 YATIN PATEL

Yatin set up a one-man architectural firm, Yatin Patel & Associates in 1989 with a modest beginning in retail projects. Within a few years Yatin Patel & Associates was busy with mega projects for Reliance and IDBI. With a vision to internationalize operations, Yatin partnered with Bimal Desai and Mehul Shah, two prominent visionaries in the architectural industry, to form DSP Design Associates Pvt Ltd in 1994. Bimal, a graduate from Manipal University, hails from a family of renowned structural consultants. He imbibes his father's strong affinity to create structures with balanced aesthetics and engineering. Mehul is extensively involved in the strategic planning of DSP Design's business expansion in the architecture related industry. His role involves business development, design, project implementation and human resources. As DSP Design Associates, the trio made rapid strides establishing a brand that is well recognized in the corporate world and leading MNCs in India. Today, DSP operates from five cities, with approximately two hundred people working for it across India.

CLIENT
I-Flex Solutions

CATEGORY
Corporate Office

LOCATION
Bengaluru, Karnataka

PRINCIPAL ARCHITECT
Yatin Patel

DESIGN TEAM
Bimal Desai

STRUCTURAL, MECHANICAL & ELECTRICAL
Cruthi
Epithilial
Power Design
Naseer Electrical

CONTRACTORS
Shapoorji Pallonji & Co Ltd

LANDSCAPE ARCHITECTS
Master Plan

PROJECT DATE
2001 – 2003

15.01 I-FLEX

Based on the client's brief of creating an iconic building, the architects planned to incorporate two main blocks, Development and Corporate, connected to the entrance of the complex. The façade is of glass and a water body surrounds the building giving it a placid appearance with a natural lake in the vicinity adding to the effect. The glazing of the façade is planned as frameless glass supported from the castellated columns on the exterior of the building by means of a tension rod system. All the glass panels are held on to the façade with spider fixtures, which are in turn held by the tension rod system. The entrance has a connecting corridor between the two buildings forms. The back drop of the entrance is a landscaped courtyard wherein a waterfall forms the point of interest. The area has a glass floor with water flowing beneath it to provide a soothing effect. Only circulation areas are planned along the glazed façade of the building so that the view outside is unrestricted. The lighting design of the interior is carefully structured to make maximum use of natural light. As per the available daylight, the light fixtures automatically reduce the light output required reducing the operational costs. Effective power saving methods and optimum air-conditioning also helps save the maintenance cost.

15.01 I-FLEX

The Development block is a three-sided building with a unique glass façade of point fixed glazing, with an expanding floor plate to lend itself the shape of a ship. Castellated steel columns are designed as architectural elements surrounding the building that have a dual function of holding the glass skin from the outside. The Corporate block is designed as a structural icon using stay cable to hold the 50 ft cantilever floor plates. The corporate block consists of a Central core of 30 ft x 30 ft RCC which houses services like the lifts, staircases, and wet blocks. 50 ft long floor plates are cantilevered from the central core that form the main office area. These floor plates are suspended back to the core by the use of tension cables. The Corporate block is designed in such a way that the usable floor plates of the building start from the third floor onwards. The central core rises majestically through the first 3 floors and enhances the cantilevered structure above. The third, fifth and the seventh floors are designed as virendel girders, which effectively form concrete boxes that are held by cables on the fourth, sixth and the terrace level.

GROUND FLOOR PLAN

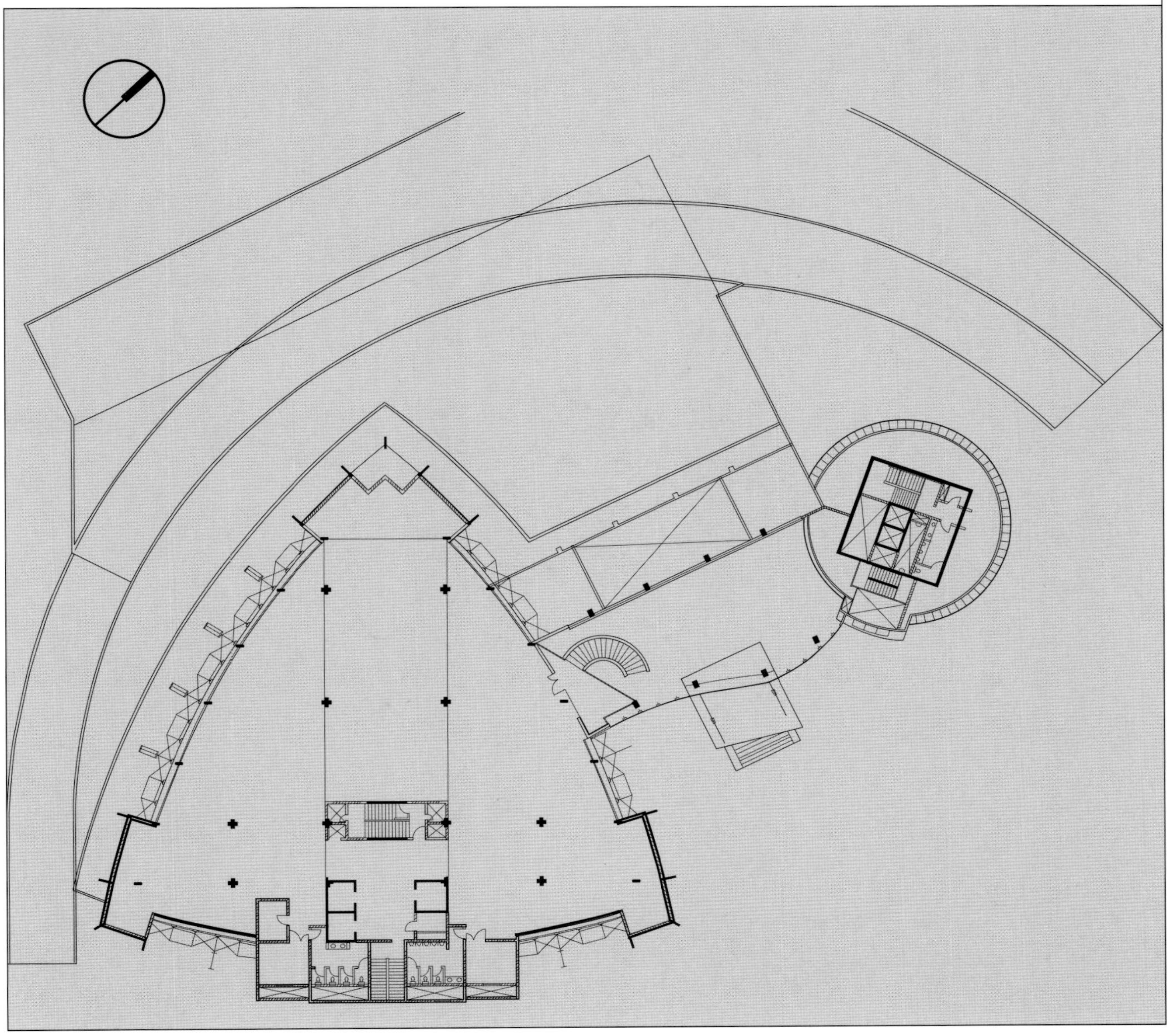

The Corporate block, which was planned as the first cable stayed structure in entire south-east Asia, had to be thoroughly detailed out architecturally, structurally and in methods of execution. The Corporate block, being cable stayed in nature, called for elaborate execution planning for casting and supporting the slabs as against a normal staging and de-staging sequence in a regular RCC building. Since the first occupied level of this building is at third floor level, staging of that height had to be erected, supported on special piles, which were specifically designed to support the staging load of eight slabs above. Once the third floor slab was cast, the staging for the fourth floor had to be erected ensuring that each staging support is exactly placed above the supports below the third floor slab to ensure proper load transfer. All slabs till the top floor were cast using the same sequence of construction without removing any staging materials from slabs below. Once the top slab was cast, the tedious and critical operations for fixing the high tensile cables began, four numbers per wing and post-tensioning the same to take the loads as per design.

logicaCMG
logicaCMG
logicaCMG

CLIENT
Logica CMG

CATEGORY
BPO

LOCATION
Bengaluru, Karnataka

PRINCIPAL ARCHITECT
Yatin Patel

DESIGN TEAM
Bimal Desai
Mehul Patel
Narendranath
Sreelaxmi
Glen Lopes

STRUCTURAL, MECHANICAL & ELECTRICAL
B L Kashyap
Micron Electricals

LANDSCAPE ARCHITECT
Master Plan

PROJECT DATE
2004 – 2005

15.02 LOGICA CMG

The brief was to design a complex that could house both software development and BPO facilities. The complex had to be a low maintenance project that could use the natural resources to the optimum. The architects began the planning of the project with the idea that simplification is the key to a beautiful building. Glazed façades within the structure's interiors provide a dual benefit; transparency within the interior design and room for natural light to filter in unobtrusively. This factor also helps the facility in achieving a certain semblance of control on its energy consumption bills. Use of particle boards and modular false ceiling components, containing recyclable content, within the entire facility also aids in achieving the green building efficiency norms. In addition, rainwater harvesting system is being used to recharge the ground water table. An acoustically treated glass façade reduces the sound level in the building. The building has effective safety measures like sprinklers and stand-by power for emergencies.

15.02 LOGICA CMG

One of the foremost challenges in the planning phase was to address the flooding of the site during Monsoon since this 1,80,000 sft site is on a low lying area with a lake present in the vicinity. To counter this situation, the whole site area was filled up to 8.2 ft and grading of the soil was professionally managed. A sub-soil drainage system was also designed for the basement of the building.

logicaCMG

logicaCMG

GROUND FLOOR PLAN

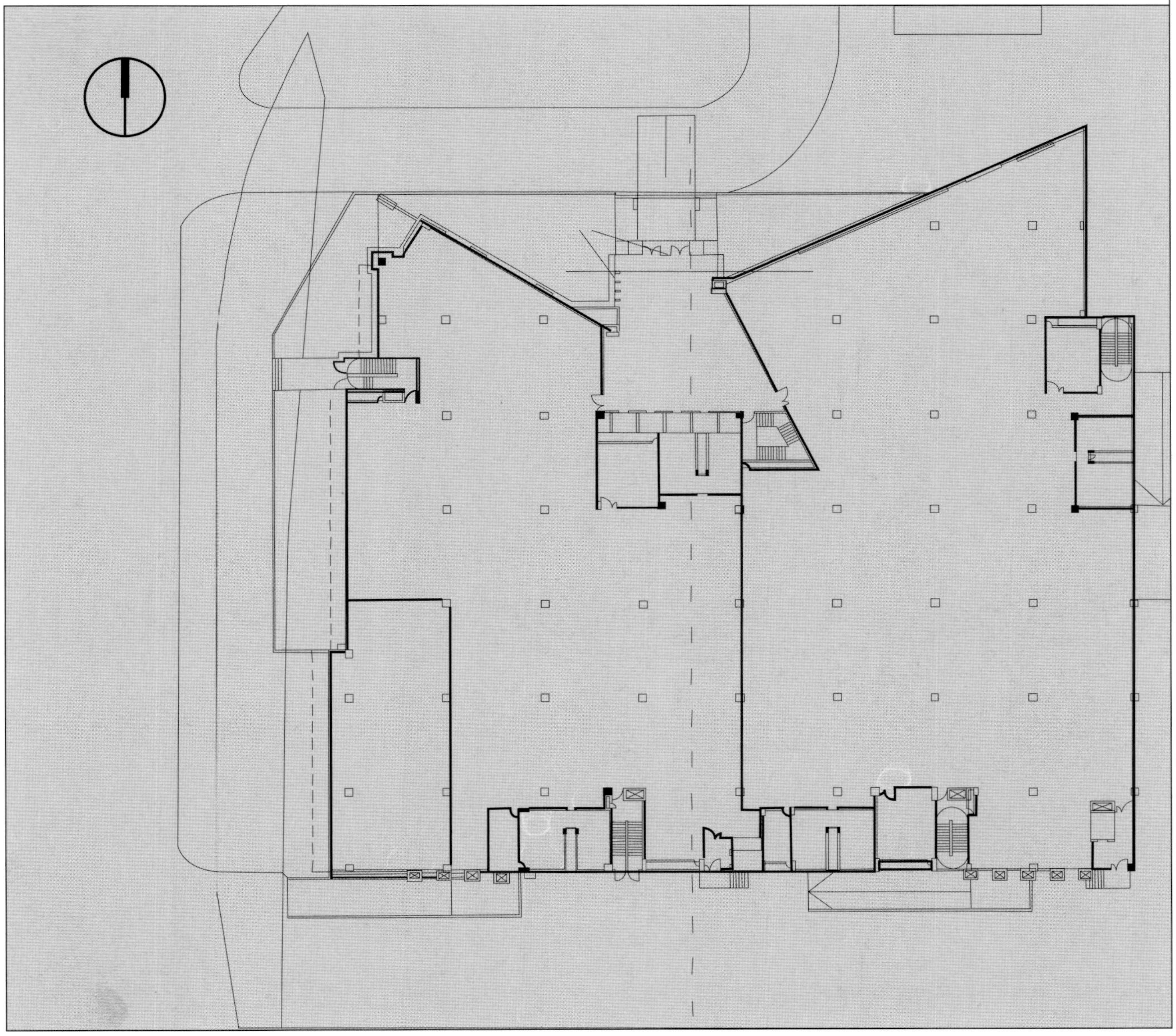

Being in close proximity to the HAL airport, the plot comes in the airport height restriction zone. Furthermore, it was necessary to cut down on the noise pollution generated by frequent taking-off and landing of aircrafts. Hence, a special glazing system was designed to derive a decibel level of 65 within the office area in the building. Double glazing with a combination of 6 mm outer glass, 24 mm insulation and 6 mm inner glass was used to cut down on decibel levels. With the exception of the northern area, where the requirement for light was greater, glazing was restricted on the faces of the building to reduce the heat intake. A flat slab structure with 1,640 ft thick capital and column spacing of 35 ft x 35 ft, forms the skeleton of this building. The building has a huge terrace cafeteria, reception and service cores among others.

acknowledgements

The management of White Flag wishes to acknowledge that "Versatile Architects of India" is the result of dedicated effort and sheer hard-work of the White Flag team. An aggressive conceptualization and coordination by the internal content team, and highly creative design inputs by Kena Design, has led this book to be a visual treat.

We are grateful to all the architects featured in this book. It is surely their contribution in terms of time and information that has made this book possible.

photo credits

COGNIZANT ARCHITECT C N RAGHAVENDRAN
EBENE CYBER TOWERS ARCHITECT C N RAGHVENDRAN

INFOSYS ARCHITECT HAFEEZ CONTRACTOR
ADITYA BIRLA HQ ARCHITECT HAFEEZ CONTRACTOR

TECHNOPOLIS ARCHITECT J P AGRAWAL
INFINITY ARCHITECT J P AGRAWAL

LUPIN RESEARCH PARK BHARATH RAMAMRUTHAM (BHARATH@GRAF.CO.IN)
INSTITUTE OF ONCOLOGICAL SCIENCES BHARATH RAMAMRUTHAM

CII SOHRABJI GBC ARCHITECT KARAN GROVER
CII ABB INSTITUTE ARCHITECT KARAN GROVER

BABULAL SANGHVI RESIDENCE SANJAY DHANIK
TIMBER VALLEY ARCHITECT NIMISH CHOKSI

EON PRASHANT BHAT
SYNTEL PRASHANT BHAT

NICHOLAS PIRAMAL RESEARCH CENTRE DINESH MEHTA
TRIKALYAM ALAN ABRAHAM (ALAN@ALANABRAHAM.COM)

GOLDEN PALMS ARCHITECT PREM NATH
CITI MALL ARCHITECT PREM NATH

INDIA EXPO MART LIMITED BHARATH RAMAMRUTHAM
ITC GREEN CENTRE BHARATH RAMAMRUTHAM, KAPIL KAMRA (KAPILKAMRA@GMAIL.COM)

RAGHULEELA MALL VINESH GANDHI (VINESH.GANDHI@GMAIL.COM)
SHIRAZI MOSQUE ARCHITECT REZA KABUL, ALAN ABRAHAM

THE OBEROI AMARVILAS OBEROI HOTELS & RESORTS
OSHO COMMUNE ADIL BHARUCHA (ADILBHARUCHA@GMAIL.COM)

AMBY VALLEY LEISURE CENTRE VINESH GANDHI
KALPATARU HORIZON VINESH GANDHI

SHIVAJI CHHATRAPATI SPORTS CITY ADIL BHARUCHA
LILAVATI HOSPITAL ARCHITECT SHASHI PRABHU

I-FLEX VINESH GANDHI
LOGICA CMG VINESH GANDHI

ORABJI GBC | CII ABB INSTITUTE | NIMISH CHOKSI | BABULAL SANGHVI RESIDENCE | TIMBER VALLEY | NITEEN PARULEKAR | EON | SYNTEL | NITIN KILLAWALA | NICHOLAS PIRAMAL R
TKI | THE OBEROI AMARVILAS | OSHO COMMUNE | SANJAY PURI | AMBY VALLEY LEISURE CENTRE | KALPATARU HORIZON | SHASHI PRABHU | SHIVAJI CHATRAPATI SPORTS CITY | LILAVA
TY | KAMAL MALIK | LUPIN RESEARCH CENTRE | INSTITUTE OF ONCOLOGICAL SCIENCES | KARAN GROVER | CII SHORABJI GBC | CII ABB INSTITUTE | NIMISH CHOKSI | BABULAL SA
ER KUMAR | INDIA EXPO MART LTD | ITC GREEN CENTRE | REZA KABUL | RAGHULEELA MALL | SHIRAZI MOSQUE | SP PATKI | THE OBEROI AMARVILAS | OSHO COMMUNE | SANJAY PU
ZANT | EBENE CYBER TOWERS | HAFEEZ CONTRACTOR | INFOSYS | ADITYA BIRLA HQ | JP AGARWAL | TECHNOPOLIS | INFINITY | KAMAL MALIK | LUPIN RESEARCH CENTRE | INSTITU
KILLAWALA | NICHOLAS PIRAMAL RESEARCH CENTRE | TRIKALYAM | PREM NATH | GOLDEN PALMS | CITIMALL | RAJINDER KUMAR | INDIA EXPO MART LTD | ITC GREEN CENTRE | REZA
JI CHATRAPATI SPORTS CITY | LILAVATI HOSPITAL | YATIN PATEL | I-FLEX | LOGICA CMG | CN RAGHAVENDRAN | COGNIZANT | EBENE CYBER TOWERS | HAFEEZ CONTRACTOR | INFOSYS
UTE | NIMISH CHOKSI | BABULAL SANGHVI RESIDENCE | TIMBER VALLEY | NITEEN PARULEKAR | EON | SYNTEL | NITIN KILLAWALA | NICHOLAS PIRAMAL RESEARCH CENTRE | TRIKAL
ILAS | OSHO COMMUNE | SANJAY PURI | AMBY VALLEY LEISURE CENTRE | KALPATARU HORIZON | SHASHI PRABHU | SHIVAJI CHATRAPATI SPORTS CITY | LILAVATI HOSPITAL | YATIN PA
LUPIN RESEARCH CENTRE | INSTITUTE OF ONCOLOGICAL SCIENCES | KARAN GROVER | CII SHORABJI GBC | CII ABB INSTITUTE | NIMISH CHOKSI | BABULAL SANGHVI RESIDENCE | TIM
ART LTD | ITC GREEN CENTRE | REZA KABUL | RAGHULEELA MALL | SHIRAZI MOSQUE | SP PATKI | THE OBEROI AMARVILAS | OSHO COMMUNE | SANJAY PURI | AMBY VALLEY LEISURE
S | HAFEEZ CONTRACTOR | INFOSYS | ADITYA BIRLA HQ | JP AGARWAL | TECHNOPOLIS | INFINITY | KAMAL MALIK | LUPIN RESEARCH CENTRE | INSTITUTE OF ONCOLOGICAL SCIENCES
AL RESEARCH CENTRE | TRIKALYAM | PREM NATH | GOLDEN PALMS | CITIMALL | RAJINDER KUMAR | INDIA EXPO MART LTD | ITC GREEN CENTRE | REZA KABUL | RAGHULEELA MALL |
ILAVATI HOSPITAL | YATIN PATEL | I-FLEX | LOGICA CMG | CN RAGHAVENDRAN | COGNIZANT | EBENE CYBER TOWERS | HAFEEZ CONTRACTOR | INFOSYS | ADITYA BIRLA HQ | JP AGAR
AL SANGHVI RESIDENCE | TIMBER VALLEY | NITEEN PARULEKAR | EON | SYNTEL | NITIN KILLAWALA | NICHOLAS PIRAMAL RESEARCH CENTRE | TRIKALYAM | PREM NATH | GOLDEN PA
PURI | AMBY VALLEY LEISURE CENTRE | KALPATARU HORIZON | SHASHI PRABHU | SHIVAJI CHATRAPATI SPORTS CITY | LILAVATI HOSPITAL | YATIN PATEL | I-FLEX | LOGICA CMG | CN R
TUTE OF ONCOLOGICAL SCIENCES | KARAN GROVER | CII SHORABJI GBC | CII ABB INSTITUTE | NIMISH CHOKSI | BABULAL SANGHVI RESIDENCE | TIMBER VALLEY | NITEEN PARULEK
E | REZA KABUL | RAGHULEELA MALL | SHIRAZI MOSQUE | SP PATKI | THE OBEROI AMARVILAS | OSHO COMMUNE | SANJAY PURI | AMBY VALLEY LEISURE CENTRE | KALPATARU HORIZON
YS | ADITYA BIRLA HQ | JP AGARWAL | TECHNOPOLIS | INFINITY | KAMAL MALIK | LUPIN RESEARCH CENTRE | INSTITUTE OF ONCOLOGICAL SCIENCES | KARAN GROVER | CII SHORAB
LYAM | PREM NATH | GOLDEN PALMS | CITIMALL | RAJINDER KUMAR | INDIA EXPO MART LTD | ITC GREEN CENTRE | REZA KABUL | RAGHULEELA MALL | SHIRAZI MOSQUE | SP PATKI
PATEL | I-FLEX | LOGICA CMG | CN RAGHAVENDRAN | COGNIZANT | EBENE CYBER TOWERS | HAFEEZ CONTRACTOR | INFOSYS | ADITYA BIRLA HQ | JP AGARWAL | TECHNOPOLIS | INFINIT
R VALLEY | NITEEN PARULEKAR | EON | SYNTEL | NITIN KILLAWALA | NICHOLAS PIRAMAL RESEARCH CENTRE | TRIKALYAM | PREM NATH | GOLDEN PALMS | CITIMALL | RAJINDER KU
E CENTRE | KALPATARU HORIZON | SHASHI PRABHU | SHIVAJI CHATRAPATI SPORTS CITY | LILAVATI HOSPITAL | YATIN PATEL | I-FLEX | LOGICA CMG | CN RAGHAVENDRAN | COGNIZANT
ES | KARAN GROVER | CII SHORABJI GBC | CII ABB INSTITUTE | NIMISH CHOKSI | BABULAL SANGHVI RESIDENCE | TIMBER VALLEY | NITEEN PARULEKAR | EON | SYNTEL | NITIN KILLAWA
SHIRAZI MOSQUE | SP PATKI | THE OBEROI AMARVILAS | OSHO COMMUNE | SANJAY PURI | AMBY VALLEY LEISURE CENTRE | KALPATARU HORIZON | SHASHI PRABHU | SHIVAJI CHATR
RWAL | TECHNOPOLIS | INFINITY | KAMAL MALIK | LUPIN RESEARCH CENTRE | INSTITUTE OF ONCOLOGICAL SCIENCES | KARAN GROVER | CII SHORABJI GBC | CII ABB INSTITUTE | NI
N PALMS | CITIMALL | RAJINDER KUMAR | INDIA EXPO MART LTD | ITC GREEN CENTRE | REZA KABUL | RAGHULEELA MALL | SHIRAZI MOSQUE | SP PATKI | THE OBEROI AMARVILAS | O
CN RAGHAVENDRAN | COGNIZANT | EBENE CYBER TOWERS | HAFEEZ CONTRACTOR | INFOSYS | ADITYA BIRLA HQ | JP AGARWAL | TECHNOPOLIS | INFINITY | KAMAL MALIK | LUPIN RE
EKAR | EON | SYNTEL | NITIN KILLAWALA | NICHOLAS PIRAMAL RESEARCH CENTRE | TRIKALYAM | PREM NATH | GOLDEN PALMS | CITIMALL | RAJINDER KUMAR | INDIA EXPO MART LTD
ON | SHASHI PRABHU | SHIVAJI CHATRAPATI SPORTS CITY | LILAVATI HOSPITAL | YATIN PATEL | I-FLEX | LOGICA CMG | CN RAGHAVENDRAN | COGNIZANT | EBENE CYBER TOWERS | HAF
ORABJI GBC | CII ABB INSTITUTE | NIMISH CHOKSI | BABULAL SANGHVI RESIDENCE | TIMBER VALLEY | NITEEN PARULEKAR | EON | SYNTEL | NITIN KILLAWALA | NICHOLAS PIRAMAL R
TKI | THE OBEROI AMARVILAS | OSHO COMMUNE | SANJAY PURI | AMBY VALLEY LEISURE CENTRE | KALPATARU HORIZON | SHASHI PRABHU | SHIVAJI CHATRAPATI SPORTS CITY | LILAVA
TY | KAMAL MALIK | LUPIN RESEARCH CENTRE | INSTITUTE OF ONCOLOGICAL SCIENCES | KARAN GROVER | CII SHORABJI GBC | CII ABB INSTITUTE | NIMISH CHOKSI | BABULAL SAN
ER KUMAR | INDIA EXPO MART LTD | ITC GREEN CENTRE | REZA KABUL | RAGHULEELA MALL | SHIRAZI MOSQUE | SP PATKI | THE OBEROI AMARVILAS | OSHO COMMUNE | SANJAY PUR
ZANT | EBENE CYBER TOWERS | HAFEEZ CONTRACTOR | INFOSYS | ADITYA BIRLA HQ | JP AGARWAL | TECHNOPOLIS | INFINITY | KAMAL MALIK | LUPIN RESEARCH CENTRE | INSTITUT
KILLAWALA | NICHOLAS PIRAMAL RESEARCH CENTRE | TRIKALYAM | PREM NATH | GOLDEN PALMS | CITIMALL | RAJINDER KUMAR | INDIA EXPO MART LTD | ITC GREEN CENTRE | REZA
JI CHATRAPATI SPORTS CITY | LILAVATI HOSPITAL | YATIN PATEL | I-FLEX | LOGICA CMG | CN RAGHAVENDRAN | COGNIZANT | EBENE CYBER TOWERS | HAFEEZ CONTRACTOR | INFOSYS
UTE | NIMISH CHOKSI | BABULAL SANGHVI RESIDENCE | TIMBER VALLEY | NITEEN PARULEKAR | EON | SYNTEL | NITIN KILLAWALA | NICHOLAS PIRAMAL RESEARCH CENTRE | TRIKAL
ILAS | OSHO COMMUNE | SANJAY PURI | AMBY VALLEY LEISURE CENTRE | KALPATARU HORIZON | SHASHI PRABHU | SHIVAJI CHATRAPATI SPORTS CITY | LILAVATI HOSPITAL | YATIN PA
LUPIN RESEARCH CENTRE | INSTITUTE OF ONCOLOGICAL SCIENCES | KARAN GROVER | CII SHORABJI GBC | CII ABB INSTITUTE | NIMISH CHOKSI | BABULAL SANGHVI RESIDENCE | TIM
ART LTD | ITC GREEN CENTRE | REZA KABUL | RAGHULEELA MALL | SHIRAZI MOSQUE | SP PATKI | THE OBEROI AMARVILAS | OSHO COMMUNE | SANJAY PURI | AMBY VALLEY LEISURE C
S | HAFEEZ CONTRACTOR | INFOSYS | ADITYA BIRLA HQ | JP AGARWAL | TECHNOPOLIS | INFINITY | KAMAL MALIK | LUPIN RESEARCH CENTRE | INSTITUTE OF ONCOLOGICAL SCIENCES
AL RESEARCH CENTRE | TRIKALYAM | PREM NATH | GOLDEN PALMS | CITIMALL | RAJINDER KUMAR | INDIA EXPO MART LTD | ITC GREEN CENTRE | REZA KABUL | RAGHULEELA MALL | S
ILAVATI HOSPITAL | YATIN PATEL | I-FLEX | LOGICA CMG | CN RAGHAVENDRAN | COGNIZANT | EBENE CYBER TOWERS | HAFEEZ CONTRACTOR | INFOSYS | ADITYA BIRLA HQ | JP AGAR
AL SANGHVI RESIDENCE | TIMBER VALLEY | NITEEN PARULEKAR | EON | SYNTEL | NITIN KILLAWALA | NICHOLAS PIRAMAL RESEARCH CENTRE | TRIKALYAM | PREM NATH | GOLDEN PA
PURI | AMBY VALLEY LEISURE CENTRE | KALPATARU HORIZON | SHASHI PRABHU | SHIVAJI CHATRAPATI SPORTS CITY | LILAVATI HOSPITAL | YATIN PATEL | I-FLEX | LOGICA CMG | CN R
TUTE OF ONCOLOGICAL SCIENCES | KARAN GROVER | CII SHORABJI GBC | CII ABB INSTITUTE | NIMISH CHOKSI | BABULAL SANGHVI RESIDENCE | TIMBER VALLEY | NITEEN PARULEKA
E | REZA KABUL | RAGHULEELA MALL | SHIRAZI MOSQUE | SP PATKI | THE OBEROI AMARVILAS | OSHO COMMUNE | SANJAY PURI | AMBY VALLEY LEISURE CENTRE | KALPATARU HORIZON
YS | ADITYA BIRLA HQ | JP AGARWAL | TECHNOPOLIS | INFINITY | KAMAL MALIK | LUPIN RESEARCH CENTRE | INSTITUTE OF ONCOLOGICAL SCIENCES | KARAN GROVER | CII SHORAB
LYAM | PREM NATH | GOLDEN PALMS | CITIMALL | RAJINDER KUMAR | INDIA EXPO MART LTD | ITC GREEN CENTRE | REZA KABUL | RAGHULEELA MALL | SHIRAZI MOSQUE | SP PATKI
PATEL | I-FLEX | LOGICA CMG | CN RAGHAVENDRAN | COGNIZANT | EBENE CYBER TOWERS | HAFEEZ CONTRACTOR | INFOSYS | ADITYA BIRLA HQ | JP AGARWAL | TECHNOPOLIS | INFINIT
R VALLEY | NITEEN PARULEKAR | EON | SYNTEL | NITIN KILLAWALA | NICHOLAS PIRAMAL RESEARCH CENTRE | TRIKALYAM | PREM NATH | GOLDEN PALMS | CITIMALL | RAJINDER KU
E CENTRE | KALPATARU HORIZON | SHASHI PRABHU | SHIVAJI CHATRAPATI SPORTS CITY | LILAVATI HOSPITAL | YATIN PATEL | I-FLEX | LOGICA CMG | CN RAGHAVENDRAN | COGNIZANT
ES | KARAN GROVER | CII SHORABJI GBC | CII ABB INSTITUTE | NIMISH CHOKSI | BABULAL SANGHVI RESIDENCE | TIMBER VALLEY | NITEEN PARULEKAR | EON | SYNTEL | NITIN KILLAWA
SHIRAZI MOSQUE | SP PATKI | THE OBEROI AMARVILAS | OSHO COMMUNE | SANJAY PURI | AMBY VALLEY LEISURE CENTRE | KALPATARU HORIZON | SHASHI PRABHU | SHIVAJI CHATRA
RWAL | TECHNOPOLIS | INFINITY | KAMAL MALIK | LUPIN RESEARCH CENTRE | INSTITUTE OF ONCOLOGICAL SCIENCES | KARAN GROVER | CII SHORABJI GBC | CII ABB INSTITUTE | NI
N PALMS | CITIMALL | RAJINDER KUMAR | INDIA EXPO MART LTD | ITC GREEN CENTRE | REZA KABUL | RAGHULEELA MALL | SHIRAZI MOSQUE | SP PATKI | THE OBEROI AMARVILAS | O
CN RAGHAVENDRAN | COGNIZANT | EBENE CYBER TOWERS | HAFEEZ CONTRACTOR | INFOSYS | ADITYA BIRLA HQ | JP AGARWAL | TECHNOPOLIS | INFINITY | KAMAL MALIK | LUPIN RE
EKAR | EON | SYNTEL | NITIN KILLAWALA | NICHOLAS PIRAMAL RESEARCH CENTRE | TRIKALYAM | PREM NATH | GOLDEN PALMS | CITIMALL | RAJINDER KUMAR | INDIA EXPO MART LTD
ON | SHASHI PRABHU | SHIVAJI CHATRAPATI SPORTS CITY | LILAVATI HOSPITAL | YATIN PATEL | I-FLEX | LOGICA CMG | CN RAGHAVENDRAN | COGNIZANT | EBENE CYBER TOWERS | HAF
ORABJI GBC | CII ABB INSTITUTE | NIMISH CHOKSI | BABULAL SANGHVI RESIDENCE | TIMBER VALLEY | NITEEN PARULEKAR | EON | SYNTEL | NITIN KILLAWALA | NICHOLAS PIRAMAL RE
TKI | THE OBEROI AMARVILAS | OSHO COMMUNE | SANJAY PURI | AMBY VALLEY LEISURE CENTRE | KALPATARU HORIZON | SHASHI PRABHU | SHIVAJI CHATRAPATI SPORTS CITY | LILAVA
TY | KAMAL MALIK | LUPIN RESEARCH CENTRE | INSTITUTE OF ONCOLOGICAL SCIENCES | KARAN GROVER | CII SHORABJI GBC | CII ABB INSTITUTE | NIMISH CHOKSI | BABULAL SAN
ER KUMAR | INDIA EXPO MART LTD | ITC GREEN CENTRE | REZA KABUL | RAGHULEELA MALL | SHIRAZI MOSQUE | SP PATKI | THE OBEROI AMARVILAS | OSHO COMMUNE | SANJAY PUR
ZANT | EBENE CYBER TOWERS | HAFEEZ CONTRACTOR | INFOSYS | ADITYA BIRLA HQ | JP AGARWAL | TECHNOPOLIS | INFINITY | KAMAL MALIK | LUPIN RESEARCH CENTRE | INSTITUTE
KILLAWALA | NICHOLAS PIRAMAL RESEARCH CENTRE | TRIKALYAM | PREM NATH | GOLDEN PALMS | CITIMALL | RAJINDER KUMAR | INDIA EXPO MART LTD | ITC GREEN CENTRE | REZA
JI CHATRAPATI SPORTS CITY | LILAVATI HOSPITAL | YATIN PATEL | I-FLEX | LOGICA CMG | CN RAGHAVENDRAN | COGNIZANT | EBENE CYBER TOWERS | HAFEEZ CONTRACTOR | INFOSYS
UTE | NIMISH CHOKSI | BABULAL SANGHVI RESIDENCE | TIMBER VALLEY | NITEEN PARULEKAR | EON | SYNTEL | NITIN KILLAWALA | NICHOLAS PIRAMAL RESEARCH CENTRE | TRIKALY
ILAS | OSHO COMMUNE | SANJAY PURI | AMBY VALLEY LEISURE CENTRE | KALPATARU HORIZON | SHASHI PRABHU | SHIVAJI CHATRAPATI SPORTS CITY | LILAVATI HOSPITAL | YATIN PA
LUPIN RESEARCH CENTRE | INSTITUTE OF ONCOLOGICAL SCIENCES | KARAN GROVER | CII SHORABJI GBC | CII ABB INSTITUTE | NIMISH CHOKSI | BABULAL SANGHVI RESIDENCE | TIM
ART LTD | ITC GREEN CENTRE | REZA KABUL | RAGHULEELA MALL | SHIRAZI MOSQUE | SP PATKI | THE OBEROI AMARVILAS | OSHO COMMUNE | SANJAY PURI | AMBY VALLEY LEISURE C
S | HAFEEZ CONTRACTOR | INFOSYS | ADITYA BIRLA HQ | JP AGARWAL | TECHNOPOLIS | INFINITY | KAMAL MALIK | LUPIN RESEARCH CENTRE | INSTITUTE OF ONCOLOGICAL SCIENCES |
AL RESEARCH CENTRE | TRIKALYAM | PREM NATH | GOLDEN PALMS | CITIMALL | RAJINDER KUMAR | INDIA EXPO MART LTD | ITC GREEN CENTRE | REZA KABUL | RAGHULEELA MALL | S
ILAVATI HOSPITAL | YATIN PATEL | I-FLEX | LOGICA CMG | CN RAGHAVENDRAN | COGNIZANT | EBENE CYBER TOWERS | HAFEEZ CONTRACTOR | INFOSYS | ADITYA BIRLA HQ | JP AGARV
AL SANGHVI RESIDENCE | TIMBER VALLEY | NITEEN PARULEKAR | EON | SYNTEL | NITIN KILLAWALA | NICHOLAS PIRAMAL RESEARCH CENTRE | TRIKALYAM | PREM NATH | GOLDEN PAL
PURI | AMBY VALLEY LEISURE CENTRE | KALPATARU HORIZON | SHASHI PRABHU | SHIVAJI CHATRAPATI SPORTS CITY | LILAVATI HOSPITAL | YATIN PATEL | I-FLEX | LOGICA CMG | CN RA
TUTE OF ONCOLOGICAL SCIENCES | KARAN GROVER | CII SHORABJI GBC | CII ABB INSTITUTE | NIMISH CHOKSI | BABULAL SANGHVI RESIDENCE | TIMBER VALLEY | NITEEN PARULEKA
E | REZA KABUL | RAGHULEELA MALL | SHIRAZI MOSQUE | SP PATKI | THE OBEROI AMARVILAS | OSHO COMMUNE | SANJAY PURI | AMBY VALLEY LEISURE CENTRE | KALPATARU HORIZON
YS | ADITYA BIRLA HQ | JP AGARWAL | TECHNOPOLIS | INFINITY | KAMAL MALIK | LUPIN RESEARCH CENTRE | INSTITUTE OF ONCOLOGICAL SCIENCES | KARAN GROVER | CII SHORAB
LYAM | PREM NATH | GOLDEN PALMS | CITIMALL | RAJINDER KUMAR | INDIA EXPO MART LTD | ITC GREEN CENTRE | REZA KABUL | RAGHULEELA MALL | SHIRAZI MOSQUE | SP PATKI
PATEL | I-FLEX | LOGICA CMG | CN RAGHAVENDRAN | COGNIZANT | EBENE CYBER TOWERS | HAFEEZ CONTRACTOR | INFOSYS | ADITYA BIRLA HQ | JP AGARWAL | TECHNOPOLIS | INFINIT
R VALLEY | NITEEN PARULEKAR | EON | SYNTEL | NITIN KILLAWALA | NICHOLAS PIRAMAL RESEARCH CENTRE | TRIKALYAM | PREM NATH | GOLDEN PALMS | CITIMALL | RAJINDER KU
E CENTRE | KALPATARU HORIZON | SHASHI PRABHU | SHIVAJI CHATRAPATI SPORTS CITY | LILAVATI HOSPITAL | YATIN PATEL | I-FLEX | LOGICA CMG | CN RAGHAVENDRAN | COGNIZANT
ES | KARAN GROVER | CII SHORABJI GBC | CII ABB INSTITUTE | NIMISH CHOKSI | BABULAL SANGHVI RESIDENCE | TIMBER VALLEY | NITEEN PARULEKAR | EON | SYNTEL | NITIN KILLAWAL
SHIRAZI MOSQUE | SP PATKI | THE OBEROI AMARVILAS | OSHO COMMUNE | SANJAY PURI | AMBY VALLEY LEISURE CENTRE | KALPATARU HORIZON | SHASHI PRABHU | SHIVAJI CHATRA
RWAL | TECHNOPOLIS | INFINITY | KAMAL MALIK | LUPIN RESEARCH CENTRE | INSTITUTE OF ONCOLOGICAL SCIENCES | KARAN GROVER | CII SHORABJI GBC | CII ABB INSTITUTE | NI
N PALMS | CITIMALL | RAJINDER KUMAR | INDIA EXPO MART LTD | ITC GREEN CENTRE | REZA KABUL | RAGHULEELA MALL | SHIRAZI MOSQUE | SP PATKI | THE OBEROI AMARVILAS |
CN RAGHAVENDRAN | COGNIZANT | EBENE CYBER TOWERS | HAFEEZ CONTRACTOR | INFOSYS | ADITYA BIRLA HQ | JP AGARWAL | TECHNOPOLIS | INFINITY | KAMAL MALIK | LUPIN RE
EKAR | EON | SYNTEL | NITIN KILLAWALA | NICHOLAS PIRAMAL RESEARCH CENTRE | TRIKALYAM | PREM NATH | GOLDEN PALMS | CITIMALL | RAJINDER KUMAR | INDIA EXPO MART LTD
ON | SHASHI PRABHU | SHIVAJI CHATRAPATI SPORTS CITY | LILAVATI HOSPITAL | YATIN PATEL | I-FLEX | LOGICA CMG | CN RAGHAVENDRAN | COGNIZANT | EBENE CYBER TOWERS | HAFE
ORABJI GBC | CII ABB INSTITUTE | NIMISH CHOKSI | BABULAL SANGHVI RESIDENCE | TIMBER VALLEY | NITEEN PARULEKAR | EON | SYNTEL | NITIN KILLAWALA | NICHOLAS PIRAMAL RE
TKI | THE OBEROI AMARVILAS | OSHO COMMUNE | SANJAY PURI | AMBY VALLEY LEISURE CENTRE | KALPATARU HORIZON | SHASHI PRABHU | SHIVAJI CHATRAPATI SPORTS CITY | LILAVAT
TY | KAMAL MALIK | LUPIN RESEARCH CENTRE | INSTITUTE OF ONCOLOGICAL SCIENCES | KARAN GROVER | CII SHORABJI GBC | CII ABB INSTITUTE | NIMISH CHOKSI | BABULAL SANC
ER KUMAR | INDIA EXPO MART LTD | ITC GREEN CENTRE | REZA KABUL | RAGHULEELA MALL | SHIRAZI MOSQUE | SP PATKI | THE OBEROI AMARVILAS | OSHO COMMUNE | SANJAY PUR
ZANT | EBENE CYBER TOWERS | HAFEEZ CONTRACTOR | INFOSYS | ADITYA BIRLA HQ | JP AGARWAL | TECHNOPOLIS | INFINITY | KAMAL MALIK | LUPIN RESEARCH CENTRE | INSTITUTE
KILLAWALA | NICHOLAS PIRAMAL RESEARCH CENTRE | TRIKALYAM | PREM NATH | GOLDEN PALMS | CITIMALL | RAJINDER KUMAR | INDIA EXPO MART LTD | ITC GREEN CENTRE | REZA K